A Man Called
MARTIN
LUTHER

KATHLEEN BENSON

Publishing House
St. Louis

To Jim

Photos in this publication are reproduced with permission of the photographer, Erwin Weber, associate professor of German, Augustana College, Rock Island, IL.

Copyright © 1980 by Concordia Publishing House
3558 South Jefferson Avenue, St. Louis, MO 63118

Library of Congress Cataloging in Publication Data

Benson, Kathleen.
    A man called Martin Luther.

    SUMMARY: A biography of the German monk who led the Protestant Reformation in Europe from its beginning in 1517 until his death in 1546.
        1. Luther, Martin, 1483-1546—Juvenile literature.
    2. Reformation—Biography—Juvenile literature.
    [1. Luther, Martin, 1483-1546. 2. Reformers]
    I. Title.
    BR325.B43   284.1'092'4 [B] [92]   80-100
    ISBN 0-570-03625-9

The world wants to deceive or be deceived. That is why the world has nothing to do with the truth.

---Martin Luther

CONTENTS

WHO WAS MARTIN LUTHER?

Martin Luther was born nearly five hundred years ago, before Columbus' voyage to America. At that time many people thought the world was flat. They did not know that things like electricity, space travel, telephones, and frozen pizzas were possible. Martin Luther was like those people. Yet his name is almost as well known today as that of Columbus. The largest branch of the Protestant Church is named after him.

In some ways Martin Luther was like Columbus. Both men took a look at their world and at what most people believed and decided that things didn't necessarily have to be that way. Columbus decided to find out more about the physical world—the land and the sea—and it is interesting to learn that he got his ideas about the nature of the world from the Bible, not from astronomy. Martin Luther decided to find out more about the spiritual world—God and where He is. Both men were explorers, both had to overcome many obstacles in their search, but of the two men, Columbus had the easier time of it. The beliefs he challenged were not as important as those that Martin Luther questioned. To prove his ideas, all Columbus had to do was to get money to outfit his ships and to hire a crew of men who were willing to risk a voyage into unknown waters. Martin Luther could not prove his ideas except to turn to the Bible. On that basis he asked people to search their own souls.

The globe has now been charted; man's soul remains uncharted. Martin Luther was exploring a world that has no limits, so he never received the honors Columbus received; his findings were never accepted as absolute truth the way those of Columbus were. Martin Luther, in fact, spent a good part of his life as a man marked for death because he knew what he believed and stuck to it but could not prove it through science or everyday experience.

He also spent a good part of his life not knowing what to believe. In his early years he was the kind of young man who today would spend a lot of his school time in the office of the school psychologist. His father and his teachers could not understand him. He didn't understand himself. He had to struggle to find out what it was he really believed in, but once he had, he never gave it up, and he publicly proclaimed his beliefs, even if it meant getting into trouble. He became famous because of his ideas and because of his determination. Not just a new church came out of his beliefs but a whole new way of thinking about man's relationship with God, with the church, with the people who have power over him.

Another man could have made the voyage Columbus did. Another man could have done what Martin Luther did. Neither Columbus nor Luther was special to begin with; both were men, not saints. But both became special, in part because history made them so and in part because of their own determination to do what they believed they had to do. Here is the story of one of those men, Martin Luther.

Chapter I.
YOUNG MARTIN LUTHER

Martin Luther was born into a world very different from the one we know today. Austria, Switzerland, and Germany were not separate and distinct countries but all part of the same empire. And everyone in the empire (except the Jews and a few scattered and persecuted groups of "heretics") belonged to the same church, the Roman Catholic Church.

Back in the late eighth and early ninth centuries Charlemagne, king of the Franks, had won control of many lands in Europe, lands where the people were uncivilized. Charlemagne decided to try to bring order and civilization to these tribes by bringing back the ancient Roman ideal of an empire. He also wanted his empire to be a Christian society. Pope Leo III in Rome liked this idea and gave Charlemagne the title Roman Emperor. After Charlemagne's descendants died out, German kings held that title, and within a few centuries all the lands controlled by a German king had come to be called the Holy Roman Empire.

By the time Martin Luther was born, that empire was known as the Holy Roman Empire of the German Nation. The change in name pointed to a desire on the part of the German kings to be more independent of Rome. It also pointed to the beginning of a sense of nationhood in Europe, although centuries would pass before the European countries would become the independent nations they are today. Germany, for example, did not even have clearly defined borders in Martin Luther's time, but the states within Germany did, and so Hans Luther, Martin Luther's father, thought of himself as a Thuringian first and as a German second.

Luther's father, Hans. Painting by Lucas Cranach the Elder, 1527. (Wartburg-Stiftung, Eisenach)

Luther's mother Margarethe. Painting by Lucas Cranach the Elder, 1527.
(Wartburg-Stiftung, Eisenach)

Hans Luther was born into a peasant family that worked the land on the estate of a nobleman. His ancestors had worked the same land on the same estate for hundreds of years. Charlemagne had set up a system in which farmers swore an oath of loyalty to a lord and bound themselves to him and his land for their lives and for the lives of their descendants. That system worked quite well unless you happened to be a son without inheritance. Since peasants usually had large families, there was the problem of how to pass on the land of the lord and the duties to him. If it was divided up equally among all the sons, none of them would have enough land to farm. So it usually went to either the oldest or the youngest. The custom in the German state of Thuringia was for the land to go to the youngest son. Hans Luther, oldest of four boys, grew up working side by side with his father and his brothers on a farm that could never be his own.

But Hans Luther was lucky. A century before, his future would have been pretty bleak. He would have faced life as a live-in servant or a farmhand for another landed peasant. Back then, almost everyone lived on farms. Now, in the late fifteenth century, there were towns where his services were needed, industries in which he could work. Through hard work and good Christian living, he believed he might even be able to rise to higher status than that of his youngest brother, who would inherit his father's land. If he saved enough money, he could buy into the burgher class. The men of this class governed the towns and the large estates of the nobility and so were higher than the peasant class.

Hans Luther married a young woman who shared his hopes and ambitions. Margaret Ziegler, who belonged to a respected peasant family in a neighboring region, was a hard worker and a religious woman who would help him to achieve his dreams. Soon after their marriage the young couple said good-by to their families and traveled about 70 miles northeast to the town of Eisleben, owned by the counts of Mansfeld. There Hans got a job working in the copper and slate mines in the foothills of the Harz Mountains. The town was divided into Old Town and New Town. New Town was where the miners lived, and this is where Hans and Margaret settled.

This is also where Martin Luther was born, probably on November 10, 1483. It is not known how long Hans and

Margaret had been in Eisleben when Martin was born, but it is known that he was their second child and that their first was probably a daughter. Not many records were kept about the lower classes then, almost none at all by the lower-class people themselves. The few records that did exist were kept by the priests and nobles and burghers. The priests kept records of baptisms, and so we know that the infant Martin Luther was baptized at Saint Peter and Saint Paul Church in Eisleben on November 11, 1483. The same baptismal font is still in that church in Eisleben, and the house where Luther was born is now a museum. The tiny boy was named for the calendar saint of that day, St. Martin of Tours.

Then, as now, in nearly every family a child was welcomed as a kind of miracle and as an extension into the future of the parents' hopes and ambitions. If Hans Luther

The house in which Luther was born on Nov. 10, 1483, in Eisleben. View from the courtyard. The building was reconstructed in 1693 and 1819.

had been the son to inherit the Luther estate, little Martin would have been looked upon as a future farm hand who would keep the lands productive. But Hans Luther was a miner in the mining community of Eisleben. His ambitions for his son were different. He hoped Martin could have enough of an education to enter a higher class. In fact, he hoped his first son could become a lawyer.

In the spring of 1484, when Martin was six months old, the Luthers moved again, closer to the Harz Mountains, to the town of Mansfeld, the center of the Mansfeld counts' mining region. Hans and Margaret Luther must have saved enough money for Hans to buy burgher rights here, for he was elected to the town council. The Luthers moved into a small, rented cottage, and Hans went about earning more money so he could buy a foundry while Margaret worked equally hard taking care of her children and tending their home, hauling firewood from the nearby forests, making candles and clothing and bed linens, cooking the family's meals. They rested only on Sundays, when they went to church.

Martin was brought up very strictly. For the smallest wrongdoing he was beaten with a switch, and his most vivid memories were not of happiness and laughter but of punishment. Children in those days were looked upon as miniature adults in many ways, and much behavior that would be considered natural today was considered unnatural in the fifteenth century.

Religious and superstitious beliefs had a lot to do with child-rearing practices. The devil was ever present, and a small child's soul was thought to be much less able than a grown-up's to fight off the devil's attacks. So anytime a child did something "devilish," it was the parents' duty to drive out the devil in him. Years later, Martin Luther would tell his students how his mother whipped him with a cane until the blood came, because he had stolen a hazelnut. Nowadays most parents would not be so harsh, realizing that the child took the nut because he wanted it and did not understand that he couldn't have everything he wanted. In Martin Luther's day, if a child stole a nut, it meant that the devil was in him, and that devil had to be beaten out.

In young Martin Luther's world, there were many forces one could not see and had little control over. The common people, especially, believed in fairies and elves and spirits and witches, and many of the fairy tales children learn today are based in German folklore. Margaret Luther was sure that such beings played tricks on her by stealing milk and eggs and butter, and her son believed the same things she did.

Even when he was grown up, Martin Luther would say in all seriousness, "Many regions are inhabited by devils. Prussia is full of them, and Lapland of witches. In my native country on the top of a high mountain called the Pulesberg is a lake into which if a stone be thrown a tempest will arise over the whole region because the waters are the abode of captive demons."

So little Martin Luther did not play freely over the hills and meadows and woods and plains of Mansfeld. He always had to keep an eye out for the spirits and beings that lived in them. And when he got home, he could never be sure if his mother would not notice something about him that made her think he had been influenced by those spirits. The arrival of younger brothers and sisters helped, for his mother was so busy with them that she did not have as much time to worry about what he was doing. But he had to be careful just the same. For by the time he was old enough to understand that there were devils and fairies and spirits lurking around to get him into trouble, he also understood that there was someone called God who was keeping track of it all.

Little Martin did not quite understand who God was, but he thought He was up in the sky somewhere, sternly watching all the bad things children did and remembering them. When bad people died, they were punished for their sins by being sent to a place called hell, where they burned forever in huge roaring fires. Often, when his mother punished him for wrongdoing, she would tell Martin she was trying to save his soul from hell. That made sense to Martin. Years later, recalling the beating he got the time he stole the hazelnut, Martin Luther would also tell his students that his mother meant well. She was not strict out of meanness but because she wanted to raise a good boy and a humble one. He would remember with a smile a little song she sang to teach her small son to be humble:

If folk don't like you and me,
The fault with us is like to be.

Young Martin minded his mother as much as he could, considering that he was an active, curious boy who often got into mischief without meaning to be bad. As his brothers and sisters began to arrive (eventually there would be seven Luther children), he was expected to help out around the house, haul firewood from the forests, and look after the younger children while his mother cooked and cleaned. But he often got distracted by an insect crawling along the ground or a bird singing in a tree or any of the numerous goings on in the neighborhood. His busy mother probably breathed a sigh of relief when Hans Luther decided to send little Martin to school.

Martin was very smart. Nothing seemed to escape his bright, dark eyes, and he asked questions about things that most other children didn't even notice. This pleased his parents, and they decided to give him a good education. There were no free schools in those times, but Hans was doing well in the mines and could afford the tuition at the Mansfeld Latin School. The quicker his son got started on his education the better, and although most boys started school at age six or seven, little Martin Luther was only four-and-a-half when he started school on St. George's Day, March 12, 1488. Because his short legs could not keep up with the other children, he was often carried on the shoulders of a neighbor boy named Nicolaus Oemler.

Mansfeld Latin School was only a few blocks from the Luther home, but it was exciting to Martin to go even that far away without his parents. Mansfeld, surrounded by hills and overlooked by the majestic castle of the Mansfeld counts, was a bustling town, full of markets and peddlers and miners on the way to and from work. There was always something to see, and though Martin enjoyed learning at school, he often thought traveling to and from school was the best part.

If anything, his teachers were more strict than his parents. Although the school was operated by the church, the priests did not teach the younger children. Instead they hired wandering university students to teach the elementary grades. The salary was very low, but poor university students would do anything for a little money to pay for their own studies. Some of them were good teachers, but many were not.

The first subject young students at Mansfeld Latin School had to learn was Latin, for it was the language of the church, of law, of diplomacy and international relations, of

14

scholarship and travel. A boy who wanted to enter any of these professions had to know Latin as well as German— better, in fact, because all the books were in Latin and all business was done in that language. The printing press had been invented only about 50 years before Martin's birth, and the first really workable press not until the 1450s, so there were very few books. Most books were still painstakingly copied by hand by monks in monasteries or by scholars or noblewomen.

The Bible was the most sought-after book and the rarest. Only the wealthiest families and churches could afford to own one, and those in libraries were usually chained to a desk or table so they could not be taken away. Martin would not see a complete Bible until he was twenty years old.

Martin and the other students worked with slates, and most of their lessons were given orally, not in books. They learned by reciting Latin words and phrases over and over

City of Mansfeld. View from the former castle of the counts of Mansfeld. The school which Luther attended is located next to the church. Luther's father's house can be seen on the right.

again, much like children today learn the multiplication tables; but they were also taught Latin through music. They were trained to sing psalms and hymns, and Martin enjoyed that. He loved music and singing and had an excellent voice. After a time he was invited to join the choir. All the students attended masses and evening services and took part in the celebrations on holy days.

As the children learned to speak Latin, they were expected to use it at all times while they were at school, and they were punished when they did not. Every day one student was appointed to spy on the others and report any of them who forgot and spoke in German. He was called the *lupus*, or wolf. At noon the student who had done most poorly on his lessons was forced to wear a donkey mask, called the *asininus*, until he caught a fellow student speaking German. The image of the donkey wearing a high "dunce" cap is familiar to many people even today.

Although Martin Luther enjoyed studying and learned quickly, he still came in for his share of punishment. Sometimes, when the weather was nice and he would have given anything to be outside rather than in the dark, damp schoolroom, he didn't pay attention to his lessons and suffered the consequences. Every time a student did something wrong, the teacher made a mark next to the student's name on a slate he kept for that purpose. At the end of the week the student would receive as many strokes of the birch whip as there were marks next to his name on the slate. His slate was then wiped clean; this is the origin of the expression, "starting over with a clean slate." Many years later Martin Luther would tell his students, "I was caned in a single morning fifteen times for nothing at all." It must be said that in telling about the incident the way he did, Luther made it seem harsher than it really was. The 15 strokes of the birch whip were punishment for 15 mistakes Martin had made during the whole week, not just in a single day. Still, Martin's early schooling was harsh, and he would later push for educational reform and speak of his own experience as "purgatory and hell."

No matter how unhappy his experiences, they did not turn Martin against learning. He did well at school and tried hard to please his teachers. When he entered the upper grades, he was asked to help tutor younger students. He rarely received marks against him on his teachers' slates, and he was thankful for that. Students in upper grades did not receive whippings. Instead they were fined, and since most of the students had no allowance, they had to get the money from their parents, which meant they got whippings anyway—at home.

As Martin grew older, he grew closer to his father. Margaret Luther was so busy with all her children that she barely had time to pray as often as she wanted to, let alone have a close relationship with any particular child. Hans Luther worked hard too, but he found time to laugh with his children and to pray with them beside their beds at night. He respected his son's intelligence and had great hopes for Martin's future, and he was not afraid to admit it when he was too harsh. As Martin Luther recalled many years later, "My father once whipped me so that I ran away and felt ugly toward him until he was at pains to win me back."

Both Hans and Martin Luther had strong ideas about things. Hans believed that because he was the father he should be respected by his son. Martin loved his father, but he didn't think he should give in to the older man just because he was his father. Martin had a way of jutting out his chin when he thought he was right. His father would get angry when he saw this. The more stubborn Martin became, the more angry his father got. Hans Luther would then punish his son for what he considered a disrespectful attitude. Martin would think he was not being treated fairly and would grow silent and moody.

All this may have been one reason why, when Martin was 14, his father decided to send him away to school: a change of environment might help his son get over his sullen ways. Hans Luther also realized his son was growing up and was no longer challenged by his studies at Mansfeld Latin School; perhaps his moodiness was due at least in part to boredom.

Martin was a little bit frightened at the idea of leaving home. He had never been away from his family before, and even though they all seemed to close in on him at times, at least he knew what to expect and what was expected of him. At the same time he was eager to be on his own. He felt that his parents treated him like a child, and he wanted desperately to show them he was no longer a child. The best way to do that was to show them he could live on his own.

17

Chapter II.
OUT ON HIS OWN

Hans Luther decided to send his son to the Cathedral School at Magdeburg, probably because a neighbor's son, John Reinecke, was also going there; and sometime in 1498 Martin and John set off for Magdeburg, traveling the 40 miles north on foot.

It was not a lonely trip. At times the roads were so thick with travelers that Martin and John had to walk along the road shoulders so the horses and ox-drawn carts could pass. Traveling peddlers who brought their wares to the remote farms and villages, groups of entertainers who performed in the towns, and parties of noblemen off to hunt passed them from both directions. The two boys saw students on their way to university towns and many young craftsmen engaged in their "wander years," a period of traveling after they had finished their apprenticeship and before they settled down.

The boys slept by the wayside or in the haylofts of farmers along the route. When they had eaten the food their parents had packed for them, they sang songs they had learned at school in return for food. Often, the people who gave them food had little more than they. The boys saw extreme poverty on their journey, in sharp contrast to the great wealth of the parties of passing noblemen riding fine horses and dressed in rich clothing. They saw hundreds of beggars, blinded and maimed by the plagues that swept through the towns every few years. They saw men who had been caught stealing bread locked into wooden stocks in the towns and the corpses of hanged criminals that were left to rot as a reminder to other people.

As they drew closer to Magdeburg, the boys were joined by hundreds of pilgrims: plowmen who had left their fields, blacksmiths who had left their forges, peasant wives who had left their kitchens to seek peace and escape from their harsh daily lives in visits to the many shrines and churches in Magdeburg, which was called a "miniature Rome." When the boys caught sight of the city, they could understand why. They had never before seen so many steeples and spires.

In addition to being a busy commercial town, Magdeburg was an important religious center. Every religious festival and holy day was celebrated there, and because all pilgrims and worshipers were expected to give money to the church, there was great wealth in the town. Many of the priests seemed more like noblemen with their rich robes and numbers of servants, and the religious processions were lavish. Seeing such a display of wealth, young Martin could better understand his father's attitude toward the church.

It is said that Hans Luther once became so ill he nearly died. The priest who came to visit him said he should make his peace with God and give all his money to the church. Hans had replied that he would give his money to his children because they needed it more. Hans Luther was not the only one who resented the wealth of the church and believed this wealth was gained at the expense of the common people. A large number of Germans felt that way. Discontent among the peasants over the money-hunger of church landlords had led to a number of local peasant revolts in the fourteenth and fifteenth centuries.

This is not to say that all the clergy were money-grubbers. The tradition of simple worship and simple living remained, but it was not as strong as it had once been. Most of the followers of that tradition had been wiped out in the 1300s, caring for the sufferers of the terrible plague that swept through Europe at that time. Men who entered the clergy after that time tended to be more interested in their own welfare than in that of their parishioners, more likely to use the fears of the common people for their own gain.

In Magdeburg Martin saw the striking contrasts of the church of his day. On the one hand, there were the wealthy priests, who ate well and lived well. On the other, there were people like Prince William of Anhalt, patron of the Franciscan monastery, who had chosen to give his life completely to God. He fasted constantly, going without food for days on end, and he roamed the streets of Magdeburg begging for food not for himself but for the poor. By the time Martin saw him, the prince, who was still a young man, was so skinny that he looked like a skeleton. "At the sight of him," Martin later recalled, "no one could keep from being moved and ashamed of his own life."

At the school Martin and his friend John had come to attend the monks followed the plainer tradition. The Order of Common Brethren stressed simple worship, without all the luxurious trappings or splendid festivals.

Although Martin had a hard schedule at the Cathedral School, he also had free time, and he enjoyed the chance to explore the city. His parents gave him money to live on, but he often sang for food anyway, proving to himself that he didn't have to depend on his parents.

The boy matured in that first year away from home, but his moodiness continued. The more he learned, the harder it was for him to decide what life was all about. He had been taught that it was just a brief period of training for the life to come, when one would either go on to eternal bliss or to everlasting damnation, but he had seen so many different ways of life. He had seen and heard talk of cruel noblemen, but all the noblemen he'd seen appeared to be blessed with wealth and status. He knew that these noblemen gave money to the church. He also knew that the church taught that giving money helped to ensure salvation. The priest had said as much to his father when his father was sick. By refusing to give his money to the church, had his father let himself in for eternal damnation? And what of the poor peasants who could not afford to give much of anything to the church: were they doomed from birth?

All people in their teen years come to realize that they will die someday, and the idea that "someday there will be no more me" is frightening. In Martin Luther's time, this fear was made worse by the vivid church teachings about hell and eternal damnation. There seemed to be few ways to avoid the worst.

Martin Luther did not even understand God the Father and Christ, for they had been presented to him as sometimes wrathful and sometimes merciful, and he had no clear picture of what caused them to be one way or the other. At times he had learned about God as the Father, at other times about the God who got so angry that He called thunder and lightning down on man. He had learned that God the Father had sent

St. Anna, patron saint of the miners. Lindenwood
sculpture by an unknown artist from Otterwisch near
Leipzig around 1530. (Museum fuer Geschichte der
Stadt Leipzig)

His Son, the Christ, to earth to die for man's sins, so Christ
seemed a bit less fearsome than His Father. But in all the
pictures Martin had seen about Judgment Day, it was Christ
who was the Judge, sentencing some souls to Paradise and
some souls to hell. To him Jesus seemed a stern discipli-
narian, not a savior and friend.

Martin had been taught that Jesus' mother, Mary, would
help people sometimes, but she could not always be counted
on, which was why Mary's mother, St. Anne, and other saints
were so often prayed to. Being more "human," they were
easier to reach. St. Anne was the patron saint of miners, and
Martin had often heard his father pray to her. Still, even with
the help of the saints, there seemed to be no guarantee of
mercy from either God the Father or Jesus the Son, and
Martin was often troubled when he looked to the future and to
death and wondered how he was going to end up on Christ's

21

right side on Judgment Day.

Martin spent just one year at Magdeburg. It is not known why Hans Luther decided to send his son elsewhere to school, but perhaps Hans and Margaret learned about their son's continuing moodiness and believed he would be better off with family. Margaret had relatives in Eisenach, to the southwest, and at the end of his first year of study at Magdeburg, Martin received word that he was to return home for a visit before going on to Eisenach, where he would finish his secondary schooling.

Martin returned home on foot, this time alone, for his friend John was to remain at Magdeburg. Although he was lonely, Martin liked the idea of making the trip by himself, for it was another proof of his independence. But he was secretly glad to get home, to eat with the family instead of singing for his supper, to be in the noisy Luther household after a year in the silent monastery at Magdeburg.

His family had prospered while he was gone. His mother no longer went to the forests to haul back bundles of firewood; now she paid a woodcutter to do it. His father proudly announced that he had saved enough money to buy a foundry and that if the foundry did well he would be able to buy a stone townhouse.

His father also spoke of his dreams for his son's future. Martin would become a lawyer and carry on the proud, hardworking tradition of the Luther family. Not many men were lucky enough to have a son as smart as Martin. Martin liked the idea that his father was proud of him, but after a time his family seemed to close in on him again. It was not long before he stopped feeling like a returning hero and started feeling again like an eldest son of whom much was expected. Martin was relieved when it came time to set off for Eisenach.

Once again Martin made a long trip on foot, alone, traveling from the Harz Mountains to the northwestern slopes of the Thuringian Forest, where Eisenach was located. A town of about 2,000 people, Eisenach was surrounded by walls and overlooked by Wartburg Castle, which by then had fallen into ruin. Young Martin liked the castle. Though crumbling, it seemed a very strong, safe place, and there was a lovely legend attached to it. It was there, according to tradition, that St. Elizabeth had given bread to the poor, and when her cruel husband had tried to catch her in the act, the bread had turned into roses and she had been saved from punishment.

Martin enrolled in the Latin School of St. George's Church. The classrooms were just as dark and damp as those in the other schools he had attended, but somehow they seemed warmer and lighter. The teachers there cared deeply about their students, and one particular teacher made a lasting impression on Martin. His name was John Trebonius, and it was his habit, when entering a classroom, to remove his hat and bow respectfully to the students. The young men were future burgomasters, chancellors, doctors, and regents, he would explain, and they deserved his respect. Understandably, Martin and his fellow students did well in that atmosphere, and later, when he became a teacher, Martin Luther carried on the tradition of respect he had first met in the classroom of Trebonius.

The church school of St. George in Eisenach which Luther attended. View from the inner courtyard toward the gothic-style walls of the former church school.

Luther or Cotta House in Eisenach. Luther is said to have lived in thie elegant half-timbered-style building. It was destroyed during World War II and now is completely rebuilt.

Martin was happy in Eisenach also because he was taken into the home of a warm and loving family there. The Cottas were friends of the Schalkes, whose young son, Henry, Martin tutored in return for his meals. Frau Cotta was so impressed with Martin that she invited him to live in their home. The Cottas were comfortably well off, for Herr Cotta was a successful businessman. Perhaps because they did not have to scrimp and save to get ahead in life, they had more time to laugh and have fun than Martin's parents seemed to have. Martin loved living with the Cottas, whose home has been preserved because it was so important to him. They and Master Trebonius helped to make Martin's three years at Eisenach among the happiest of his life.

Those three years were for Martin like an oasis in a desert of uncertainty, for he had been bothered by doubts before Eisenach and would continue to be disturbed by them after he left. Who was God and who was Jesus? How come some people were rich and others poor? Why was life easy for some people and hard for others? In some ways his doubts were the same as those that plagued Germany and to a certain extent the rest of Europe at that time. Especially in the Holy Roman Empire of the German Nation there was such upheaval and unrest that more and more people were forecasting doom, for a world without order could not survive. Many people believed that the world would end on New Year's Day of 1500.

Aware of this possibility, a man named Hartmann Schedel in Nuernberg had decided it was a good idea to write a history of the world so surviving generations, if any, would know what man had done before them. He started with Adam and Eve and ended with Judgment Day. The huge volumes were published in June 1493. In March 1493 Christopher Columbus had returned from his voyage to the new world, but news traveled slowly in those days, and Schedel probably had never heard of Columbus when he published his history. He probably did know about the discovery of the Cape of Good Hope at the tip of southern Africa in 1488, but he did not seem to think that discovery had much to do with the condition of the world as he knew it.

Actually, both discoveries would have a lot to do with the condition of the European world. The idea that there was more world across the wide oceans would spark the imaginations of many Europeans and give them something to think about besides their own problems. The fact that there was more world beyond the seas would take some of the pressure off the European social order, for people without land and without hope could be sent to colonize the new territories. It would also take some of the pressure off the European economic system, for the riches of the new lands would fill the treasuries of the church and the nobility and the rising merchant class, and they would no longer have to depend on wars and on heavy taxation of the peasants for their income. All this was a long way off, but the possibilities were enormous.

Like most Germans, Martin Luther was not aware of these possibilities. All he knew was that New Year's Day 1500 came and went without the world ending, and he entered the last semester of high school quite as confused as ever as to what life was all about.

Chapter III:
A BIG DECISION

Whenever an important visitor came to St. George's School, one of the best students was selected to give a welcoming speech. Martin was chosen when Professor Jodocus Trutvetter of the University of Erfurt came to visit. Martin's speech, in Latin of course, impressed the professor so much that he urged Master Trebonius to prepare the boy for the University of Erfurt and told Martin he should enroll there when he finished his studies at St. George's. Martin remembered that day, and when he graduated from St. George's in the spring of 1501, he asked his father to send him to Erfurt.

Hans Luther could afford to send his son to college. He had continued to prosper in Mansfeld, would soon own several foundries, and would buy a stone townhouse there. He had no quarrel with his son's choice of the University of Erfurt, for it was considered one of the best universities in Germany. After a brief visit with his family, Martin traveled to Erfurt to begin his college career.

A little closer to Mansfeld than Eisenach, and further to the east, Erfurt was a great center for the dye industry. The city was surrounded by fields of yellow saffron and woad, grown for its blue dye extract, as well as meadows of blue-flowered flax. Erfurt also had many steeples and spires, for it was an important religious center. The cathedral and church of St. Severus, standing side by side on a hill called the Domberg, dominated the city, and one of the busiest areas was the Merchant Bridge, lined with houses and shops.

The university had been founded in 1392. It had about 2,000 students taking a variety of courses when Martin Luther enrolled in May 1501 to begin his studies in the faculty

Jodocus Trutvetter, one of Luther's professors at the University of Erfurt. From the Student Registration Book No. II, 1498—1600, of the University of Erfurt. (Stadtarchiv, Erfurt)

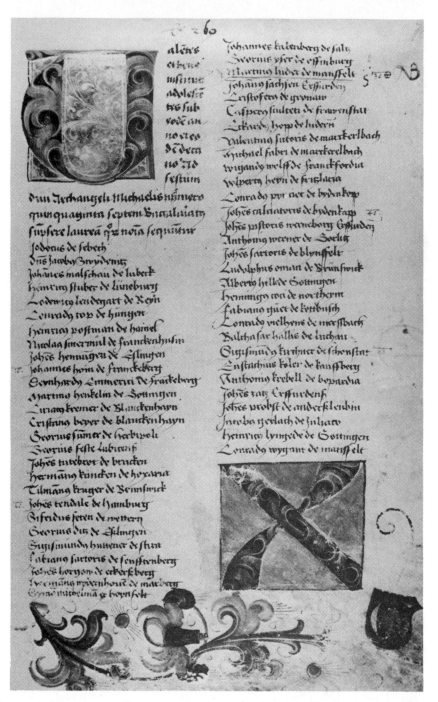

Luther's name is recorded in the Student Registration Book No. II, 1498—1600, of the University of Erfurt: "Martinus Luder de Mansfelt." (Stadtarchiv, Erfurt)

City of Erfurt. View toward the cathedral in which Luther was ordained to the priesthood on April 4, 1507.

of fine arts. It had dormitories where the students lived (Martin stayed in the Burse of St. George) and so many buildings that it took him awhile to find his way around. In Eisenach there had only been about 2,000 people in the whole town, and here he was at a university with that many students! They came from all over Germany, and at first Martin was lonely among so many strangers. After a time he met other students from Thuringia, and he sometimes visited Professor Trutvetter, but he still had trouble getting used to university life that first year. He made only average grades in his studies, and when he received his Bachelor of Arts degree in 1502, he was 30th in a class of 57. Still, he had earned the degree and with it the right to wear the academic sword that was a symbol of his new status. He proudly returned home to show his family he had lived up to their hopes.

On the way he managed to trip and drive the sword through his leg. The friend he was traveling with rushed back to Erfurt to find a doctor, but by the time help arrived, Martin nearly bled to death, for the blade had cut through a major artery. Carried back to the city by cart, he tossed and turned in bed for days, racked with fever. The infection traveled to his foot and caused it to swell. In his moments of consciousness Martin Luther was sure he would die and just as sure that he was not ready. He was terrified at the prospect of death, for he did not feel that in his brief life he had earned salvation.

He did not die. But he lost so much blood that he was very weak. It was months before he fully recovered. During this time he learned how to play the lute, a guitarlike instrument. He also did a lot of thinking about his accident, his fear of death, and his religion. When he returned to classes, to study for a Master of Arts degree, he began to read as much as he could about philosophy.

As college students have always done, Martin and his friends spent a great deal of time talking about what they were learning, exchanging ideas and trying to outtalk one another. Nowadays such get-togethers are called "bull sessions." In Martin Luther's time they were a lot more formal than they are now. A few friends would form a group based on shared interests and run it like a club. Martin's group was called the "poets" because they were interested in writing. They met regularly to read and talk about each other's work. After his accident Martin turned more to philosophy, and soon his friends started to call him "the Philosopher," because nearly all his writings and criticisms of others' writings were from that standpoint.

Several different philosophies were popular in Europe at the turn of the 16th century, and because life was so closely tied to religion, they were mostly religious philosophies. One traditional philosophy held that reason could be applied even to matters of faith, such as the existence of God. Martin Luther could not agree with that philosophy, because every time he tried to prove through reason or common sense that God existed, he failed. Martin found a philosophy called the "New Way" easier to understand. According to this philosophy reason could be applied to some problems in religion, but when it came to matters of faith, such as the existence of God, reason was bound to fail. True knowledge of such things could come only through revelation, that is, the Bible or (as people thought then) the authority of the church.

Martin underwent a kind of revelation while at the University at Erfurt: he saw a complete Bible and actually read part of it. It was chained to a desk in the library, and he found it quite by accident, for he had not been assigned to read it. He was studying fine arts, not theology; but even if he had been a religion student he would not have been encouraged to read it. Theology students were taught from postils, or written commentaries on the Bible, not from the Bible itself, and thus young Martin Luther, who had been brought up in a religious family and gone to schools run by the church nearly all his life, knew the Bible not at all.

Years later he told about his discovering that great book: "Thirty years ago no one read the Bible, and it was unknown to all people. The prophets were unknown and not even understandable. When I was twenty years old, for example, I still had never seen a Bible. I was under the impression that no other Gospel or Epistle [Letter] existed except for those recorded in the Sunday postils. Finally I found a Bible in the university library and read a passage in the book of Kings (1 Sam. 1) dealing with the mother of Samuel. The book appealed to me in a wonderful way, and I knew that I would consider myself fortunate if I could some day own such a book. . . . But then the sound of the bell summoned me to my class lecture."

Reluctantly Martin closed the Bible and went to his class, but he went back to the library as often as he could after that to turn the book's pages carefully and to pause here and there to read a passage. Nowadays, when everyone can have a Bible, it is hard to understand how Martin Luther felt or how it might be never to have seen a Bible before. The Bible was not a secret document; Martin did not feel as if he was doing anything sneaky by going to the library to read it. It was just that the Bible was not the basis for the kind of religion taught by the church in the early 16th century. The teachings of the church were based on the ideas of the church. Bibles were scarce, and reading the Bible was not considered important.

Martin's discovery of the Bible did not bring about any

31

great change in him. The book interested him, but he was so unfamiliar with it that he had no idea where to start reading. Of course the logical place to start any book is at the beginning, but as anyone knows who has tried to start reading the Bible from page one and does not know that it gets good later, all those "begats" can get pretty confusing and pretty boring. Martin's search for God and for the meaning of life was still not focused at this time. He had practically forgotten his terror at being so sick after his accident, and everyday things, like his friends and his studies, occupied his mind.

A plague swept through Erfurt in the spring of 1505. The classrooms at the university quickly emptied as students either became ill or went home to try to escape the dread disease. Black crosses were placed on the doors of many homes in the city, a sign that the plague had struck those homes. A close friend of Martin's died, and once again Martin, who did not go home, felt the nearness of death. But plagues were common in Germany and in the rest of Europe, and it did not cause normal activity to cease altogether, nor did it dim the ceremony at which Martin Luther and his classmates were awarded the master's degree.

"What a magnificent sight the conferring of the master's degree was, with the torches leading the procession," Martin would recall many years later. "I don't believe that any worldly celebration could equal it." This time Martin Luther was second out of a class of 17.

Now that Martin had received, or had been "donned" with, his master's cap, he was a member of a very special group in Germany. Not many young men were lucky enough to receive the kind of education he had been given. He was automatically entitled to respect, and from then on his father would not address him with the familiar *du* but with the more formal *Sie*.

Martin was now qualified to teach, and he was offered a job teaching at Erfurt, but he knew more was expected of him. He was supposed to go on to study law. When he was granted his master's degree, his father proudly presented him with a copy of the *Corpus Juris*, or Body of Law. If Martin had told his parents about his desire to have a copy of the Bible, they would not have taken it seriously.

Martin began to attend lectures in law at the University

of Erfurt. He lasted just two months. He was not interested in law. He did not know exactly what he was interested in, but he knew it was not law, and he thought it was a waste of his time and his father's money to continue in that course of study. He decided to return home to Mansfeld and have a talk with his father.

Hans Luther was surprised to see his son and shocked and angered when he heard what Martin had to say. Almost from the moment of Martin's birth, Hans had made plans for him. He would be educated and become a lawyer and marry a girl from a well-to-do family. Hans had seen those plans become reality: his son had earned his master's degree and had started to study law; and Hans had found a young girl from a good family for his son to marry. Now, all of a sudden, Martin was wrecking his plans. Hans Luther refused to listen to his son's doubts. The very idea that he could have doubts angered the older man, who had always been too busy working to have time for doubts. He ordered his son back to Erfurt.

Martin left home angry and confused. He had been unable to persuade his father that a career in law was not for him. In fact, his father was convinced only that Martin was a troublesome burden who did not appreciate all the opportunities he had been given. Martin felt he had failed his father and himself—especially himself, for here he was on his way back to Erfurt to continue studying for a career he did not want. But the other choice was even worse: he could not bear to leave his family, to go off on his own and do what he wanted to do, disregarding their wishes. There seemed no way out, he muttered to himself as he stumbled along the road south, wondering if he could have presented his case at home better, dreading the years of study ahead of him.

As Martin neared Erfurt on a warm, gray day, the gathering dark clouds seemed to reflect his stormy mood. Rather than seek shelter in the nearby village of Stottern-heim, he plodded on as the raindrops began to fall and the rumblings of thunder came nearer. He was so depressed that he hardly cared what happened to him at that point. But he quickly changed his mind when the storm struck. As thunder crashed and lightning bolts seemed to shoot out of the sky directly at him, all the horrible images of Judgment Day seemed to come alive around him, and he was terrified. He fell to the ground and cried out to St. Anne, "Save me and I shall become a monk!"

Not long afterward the storm passed, leaving Martin soaked but unharmed. He continued on to Erfurt, thinking about the pledge he had made, wishing he hadn't made it. He had never seriously thought about becoming a monk. He liked the idea even less than the idea of a career in law. But since he had been saved from the storm, he felt he could not forget his frightened promise. Although people were much more afraid of God then, because they believed He was a

At this place Luther is supposed to have said, "Help me, St. Anna, I want to become a monk." The marker indicates that with a bolt of lightning young Luther was shown the road to the Reformation. It is located approximately one-half mile from the village of Stotternheim.

wrathful God, not every promise offered was kept. People made all sorts of pledges in moments of fear or piety, then forgot them or sadly decided it was impossible to make good on them, just as people do today. Martin thought of doing other things that might please St. Anne, like making a pilgrimage to one of her shrines or giving money to the church in her name. But he knew he would feel guilty if he did not keep his word, and he was afraid of what would happen to him if he went back on his promise.

Besides, the more he thought about what to do the more he realized his future looked pretty bleak anyway. If he became a monk, he would not have to make any more decisions about his life, for his path would be laid out for him. And becoming a monk would solve another of his problems— the problem of how to escape hell and damnation. If he became a monk, he would no longer have to worry about dying. So, though his reasons were not the best, Martin Luther decided to keep his promise to St. Anne.

When he told his teachers and his friends of his decision, they couldn't believe it. How could a student with so much promise and such a bright future ahead of him give it all up for life in a monastery? Martin told them he was "trying to get a gracious God." He probably meant that he wanted to prove his worthiness to God, so that He would look graciously on him.

That his teachers opposed his plan troubled Martin, but he knew their opposition was mild compared with what his father's would be. He decided not to go home to tell his father but tell him by letter. By the time he would have his father's reply, he would already be in the monastery, and there would be no going back.

Martin gave his worldly goods to his friends. His books, including the brand-new copy of the *Corpus Juris* his father had so proudly given him, he sold to a bookseller. On the evening of July 16, 1505, he invited his friends to a farewell dinner, and the following morning they went with him to the monastery of St. Augustine at Erfurt. He turned to wave good-by to them; then the gate that divided the world of the monastery from the outside world closed him in. "I never intended to leave the monastery," he said many years later. "I had died completely to the world." At the time he was not yet 22 years old.

Chapter IV.
BROTHER MARTIN

In the world of Luther's time religion was an important part of life, and life itself was thought of as a short time of preparing for the hereafter. With this in mind many people chose to practice religious works that went beyond those expected of the average person. They devoted their whole life to God, expecting to be better off than others in the life to come. Most of these people joined together in societies that separated themselves from the outside world and gave up most connections with that world. Inside the monasteries for men and the convents for women life centered in prayer and meditation and study.

Some monasteries were quite wealthy, for they owned land and collected taxes from the peasants who lived on it and farmed it. Others were quite poor. Some orders (groups of monasteries following particular rules and philosophies) were stricter than others. The one Martin Luther decided to enter was a strict one. The Augustinian Order of Hermits, founded in Italy in 1287, was named after St. Augustine, a great monk who lived from 354 to 430.

During his first two months at the monastery Martin was given a chance to think over his decision to become a monk. Such decisions were not made lightly, and the Augustinian brothers wanted Martin to be sure. It was not unusual for young men who were emotionally upset or not getting along with their families or dissatisfied with their way of life to seek escape from their problems in a monastery without having felt a true calling to give their lives to God. So those who arrived at the monastery were given a chance to change their minds. Martin stayed in a guest room, and though he was allowed to take part in some of the activities of the monastery, he was kept separate in many ways. During this time he received an angry letter from his father, who refused to give his blessing to his son's decision. Martin wanted very much to have his father's approval, but he wasn't going to let anything stop him from becoming a monk. By September 1505 he had convinced the Augustinian brothers that he was sincere, and they invited him to become a novice in the order.

All the monks gathered in the monastery chapel for the ceremony. The prior, or head of the monastery, stood on the steps of the altar. Martin stepped forward and knelt as the

Main portal of the monastery church of the Augustinian Order of Hermits in Erfurt. The church was destroyed during World War II and has been completely rebuilt, as well as other buildings of the monastery, after the air attack on Feb. 25, 1945.

prior questioned him: Did Martin have any ties to or un-finished business in the world outside? Did he understand the hardships of the monastic life, and was he willing to accept them? Martin gave the right answers to these questions. Then, as the choir chanted, the monks shaved a circle of hair from the crown of his head and gave him a skullcap; he took off his worldly clothing and put on the habit of the order, a white robe under a leather-belted black cloak. Then he knelt again before the altar as the prior prayed for him; and as the choir sang the closing hymn, he fell to the floor and stretched out his arms so that his body formed the shape of a cross. He prayed for God's grace and for the strength to be worthy of it. The other monks helped him to his feet and welcomed him into the order, and Martin felt peace inside himself, felt as if he belonged. But in case he felt that was all there was to becoming a monk, he was quickly reminded that he was only a novice and that the next year would be a further testing period. The prior spoke these final words: "Not he that has begun, but he that endures to the end shall be saved."

Many years later Luther said that during the first year in the monastery the devil is very quiet. By this he meant that during his first year his mind was peaceful and his doubts disappeared. He found peace in the routine of the cloister, where life was measured by bells. The rising bell would sound at 2 a.m., and Martin would get up from his small, hard bed, make the sign of the cross, put on his white robe and skullcap, and make his way to the chapel for prayers. Six more times each day a bell would sound, and the monks would gather in the chapel to pray.

There were periods of work, scrubbing the stone walls and floors, preparing the monks' meals in the kitchen, tending the monastery gardens; periods of study, periods of strict silence, and periods when the monks were allowed to talk quietly with one another. Each monk spent a great deal of time in his small, sparsely furnished cell in private communication with God, praying, reading, and meditating.

No novice worked harder than Martin Luther did that year. In part this was because he was treated very strictly by the full-fledged monks. They thought he might be guilty of pride because he was educated, and they gave him the dirtiest and hardest jobs, hoping to crush any pride left in him. Martin did whatever he was told without complaining. He was far harder on himself than anyone else could be: he prayed on his knees on the cold floor of his cell longer than the rules asked for; he fasted, or went without food, many days longer than was necessary, so long, in fact, that he grew skinny and hollow-looking. The other monks were amazed at such devoutness and dedication on the part of such a young man, and when Martin's year as a novice ended, there was no question that he be accepted as a full-fledged member of the order. His superiors probably suspected that he was trying too hard, driving the doubts from his mind through sheer physical and mental force, but they realized that his intenseness and his energy might be fruitful if directed properly. At the end of the year, there was another special ceremony when Martin took his final vows and pledged his life to serving God as a full brother of the Augustinian order.

There were two divisions in the order, the clergy and the laity. Those who were quick learners were chosen for the clergy, and not long after he was admitted as a full brother, Martin was told he had been chosen to study for the priesthood. He was a natural choice because of his education, but perhaps his superiors also hoped that further education and his duties in the priesthood might take his mind off his passionate wrestling with himself for the salvation of his soul.

As a candidate for the priesthood Martin came into contact with John von Staupitz, vicar general of the Augustinians in Germany and a professor of theology at the University of Wittenberg. Staupitz was interested in the serious young monk, and Martin thought of Staupitz as both an adviser and a substitute for the father who had refused to accept his independence and his ability to make his own decisions.

Because of his studies Martin no longer had to do as much work around the monastery. He read a great deal about the mass and how it was used in the worship of God. Sometimes he was excited by what he read, but sometimes he was frightened by it. A priest was supposed to be closer to God than any other man except the pope. He alone could say the almost mystical rites of the mass. No one else, not even an emperor or a king, could perform the miracle of transforming the altar bread and wine into the flesh and blood of the Lord Jesus. Not even the angels had such power. If a priest performed his duties properly, it seemed to Martin, he was

John Staupitz, prior of the Augustinian Order of Hermits. He was also professor of theology at the University of Wittenberg 1502—12. Painting by an unknown artist. (Monastery St. Peter of the Benedictine Order of Monks in Salzburg)

almost assured of salvation.

But a priest stood before God without protection. Other men could talk to God through the priest; the priest had no one between himself and God. Martin was not sure he was ready to talk to God directly. How could he, a miserable sinner, dare to approach God? As the time for Martin to say his first mass drew nearer, he became even more frightened. It was supposed to be a celebration, a marking of his coming-of-age as a priest. Even his father would be there; in fact the date of Martin's first mass was postponed a month so his father could come.

In May 1507 Hans Luther set out for Erfurt with an escort of 20 horsemen. He'd had little contact with his son since Martin had entered the monastery. The monks and especially the novices were not supposed to have much contact with the outside world, and Hans Luther had not been all that anxious to see the son who he felt had betrayed him. But over the years a plague had swept through Germany, and Hans's two other sons had died. Martin was now his only son, and so Hans tried to put aside his resentment and make the best of the situation. There were those who thought he was lucky to have such a son, and since Hans Luther did not want those people to wonder about him, he went to a lot of trouble to show a pride he did not really feel. He gathered an impressive group of fine horsemen, caused a lot of excitement as he and his horsemen entered Erfurt, and made a large cash gift to the monastery to show both his wealth and his generosity. Hearing of the gift, Martin dared to hope that his father had changed his mind at last.

Now all Martin had to worry about was the mass. He had read and reread the manuals and told himself he had nothing to fear. The manuals were so careful to tell him not to be afraid that he realized he was not the first new priest to be frightened. No mistake was fatal, he had read; the sacrament would be effective as long as he performed it with the right intention. Before celebrating the mass, he would confess and receive absolution for his sins, but even if in the middle of the celebration he suddenly remembered some deadly sin he had forgotten to confess, he should continue, knowing he could receive absolution afterward. Even if he lost his voice, an older priest would be there to carry on. Martin Luther realized there was really no way he could destroy the mass, so on that day in May 1507 as he approached the altar he was nervous but not terrified.

In a voice that sounded much calmer than he felt, he began to say the introductory part of the mass, and his nervousness began to leave him. After all, he had practiced hundreds of times. But when he reached the words, "We offer unto Thee, the living, the true, the eternal God," his voice left him completely. He thought to himself, "With what tongue shall I address such Majesty, seeing that all men ought to

41

tremble in the presence of even an earthly prince? Who am I, that I should lift up mine eyes or raise my hands to the divine Majesty? The angels surround Him. At His nod the earth trembles. And shall I, a miserable little pygmy, say, 'I want this, I ask for that'? For I am dust and ashes and full of sin, and I am speaking to the living, eternal, and true God."

Martin looked about him and realized he had to go on. He could not disgrace himself in the eyes of his father and his friends. After what seemed to him like ages but was really only a few moments, he managed to get his voice back and finish the mass. The people attending the mass barely noticed the break in the service.

The mass completed, Martin was congratulated by his superiors and fellow monks, and a reception was held to celebrate the event. During the celebration dinner he sat with his father, who congratulated his son but did not seem very enthusiastic. Hoping to put his father's mind at ease, Martin told him, "My new life is so quiet and godly." It was the worst thing he could have said. Hans Luther had looked forward to a quiet retirement, his foundries operated by his sons. Now two sons were dead, and Martin, in Hans Luther's eyes, was as good as dead. "You learned scholar," he thundered, "have you never read in the Bible that you should honor your father and your mother? And here you have left me and your dear mother to look after ourselves in our old age."

Although his father's words hurt, Martin replied calmly, "But Father, I could do you more good by prayers than if I had stayed in the world." He then reminded his father that he had been called by a voice from heaven out of a thunder cloud. But Hans Luther was still not sure Martin's vision had been real. "God grant," said Hans, "that it was not a trick of the devil."

That remark made Martin feel even worse because it put into words his own fears, though he rarely admitted them to himself. Deep inside his soul, he himself was not even sure his vision had been real. The devil was real; he believed that, as did everyone else. There was God and there was the devil, and the devil was known to disguise himself as an angel of light in order to lead men astray. Martin was pretty sure he had not followed a false vision, but there was always that nagging doubt. Relieved that his first mass and his father's visit were over, he plunged back into his search for salvation, hoping by sheer hard work to quiet the doubt that his father's remark had stirred.

Many altars in the Erfurt area were served by the Augustinians, and Martin went to these churches to say the mass whenever he could. Although he still felt unworthy of such direct contact with God, at the same time he believed that this kind of contact would bring him closer to salvation. Later he would remark that he had become a "slave" of the mass. He also studied very hard. Recognizing how bright Martin was, the prior of the monastery arranged for Martin to return to the University of Erfurt to study for a bachelor's degree in Bible studies. The degree would prepare him to give introductory lectures on the Bible.

Most of the students Martin had known at the university had completed their degrees and left. Those who remembered him at all hardly recognized him. He was very thin; his cheekbones jutted out from his face and his cheeks were deep hollows beneath them. His eyes seemed darker and more piercing, and he looked far older than his 24 years.

In the monastery he continued to fast for days on end, to pray much longer than was required, and to spend entire winter nights lying on the cold stone floor of his cell. Years later he remarked, "If any monk ever got to heaven through monkery, then I too should have made it. All my monastery companions who knew me will testify to that. In fact, if it had lasted much longer, I would have killed myself with vigils, praying, reading, and other labors."

Fortunately, Martin Luther was not to remain in the monastery at Erfurt. In the fall of 1508 John von Staupitz visited the cloister, as he had done regularly since becoming vicar general of the Augustinians in 1503. This time he had come just to see Martin Luther. He needed a temporary instructor to teach philosophy at the University of Wittenberg, and although Martin had not yet earned his degree at the University of Erfurt, Staupitz believed he could handle the job.

Over the years Martin had come to admire and respect Staupitz. He was pleased that the older man believed in his ability. Although he was not sure he wanted to leave the monastery at Erfurt (for the monastery at Wittenberg had much more relaxed rules), he began to see the change as a chance to prove that he could keep his order's strictness even in a more casual atmosphere. He agreed to take the job.

Chapter V.
LUTHER VISITS ROME

Wittenberg, about 100 miles northeast of Erfurt, was little more than a village compared with Erfurt. Its population was somewhere between 2,000 and 2,500, and the whole length of the town was only nine-tenths of a mile. It was practically an island, since it was bounded by the Elbe River on one side and by a manmade moat on the other. It had an excellent harbor, and though it was built on a sand belt, its land was productive. Grain, vegetables, and fruit grew well.

Until 1502 the most important building in Wittenberg had been the Castle Church. But in that year the Elector Frederick the Wise (one of the six princes and archbishops who could vote to elect the emperors) had founded the University of Wittenberg, and its buildings would eventually become the most important in town. Frederick hoped his university, whose teachers were members of the Augustinian order, would become as important as the century-old University of Leipzig, but in its first six years the institution had not lived up to his hopes. It was new, as yet unfinished, and could not hope to be respected like the much older institution. Martin Luther was probably glad to have his first teaching position in a small, new university where there were no old and firm traditions.

Luther moved into the Augustinian cloister at the opposite end of town from the Castle Church; his small cell was much like his cell at the Erfurt monastery. The cloister was still not finished, but Luther learned to get used to spending his time in unfinished buildings. The university itself had only one completed structure. Students went to classes in the elector's castle and in the cloister. Students and faculty attended services at the Castle Church, but even it was incomplete. In 1490 Frederick had decided to rebuild it, and the work was not yet finished when Martin Luther arrived.

Although these conditions were not the easiest to live and work under, they did give a pioneering, adventurous air to

The elector of Saxony, Frederick the Wise. Bronze grave marker by Peter Vischer the Younger, 1527. The casting is a masterpiece of the early German Renaissance period. The head is an excellent likeness of the electoral prince. (Castle Church, Wittenberg)

the university and the activities that went on there. Unfortunately Luther was too much taken up with other things to notice or share in it. For a while he was so busy getting used to his new surroundings, his new job, and his students that he forgot about his own troubles. But soon his doubts and worries returned. He began to wonder if he was fit to be a teacher of moral philosophy when he was so full of sin himself. Salvation seemed as far away as ever, and once again he began fasting too long, locking himself in his room as punishment, flagellating, or beating, himself, spending such long hours confessing his sins that his tired confessor would sometimes exclaim, "Man, God is not angry with you. You are angry with God. Don't you know that God commands you to hope?" The other monks were sometimes afraid he would do himself real harm (they once broke down the door to his cell after he had been locked in there too long and found him unconscious on the floor). At other times they just felt exasperated with him for being so self-centered.

John von Staupitz could also become impatient with his young friend. Luther was such an intelligent, sensitive man who tried so hard. Staupitz was troubled by his refusal to accept the good qualities in himself. Staupitz had a different view of God and salvation than Luther did. He saw God as loving and the way to salvation as simply accepting God's love. Arrogance, pride, ego—everything connected with self—had no place in the worship of God, Staupitz believed, and he tried to tell Luther that his very striving was keeping him from the salvation he sought. It was as if Luther was trying to force God to recognize him. He was making religion much too hard work. But Luther could not understand Staupitz's view. He had grown up with the idea of a wrathful God, and he stubbornly held on to it.

Staupitz tried reminding Luther of the Gospel of Jesus Christ: that God had loved the world enough to send His own Son to die for man's sins. Couldn't Martin view Jesus Christ as his Savior too? But Luther could not. He saw Christ as a judge sending souls to damnation. To him Christ was just as rigid and unforgiving as God the Father, so he listened respectfully to what Staupitz had to say and went right on believing as he always had.

While teaching at Wittenberg, Luther was also a student. In March 1509 he earned the bachelor's degree in Bible studies. Seven months later he was called back to Erfurt to teach at the university. He moved back into the Augustinian monastery at Erfurt, taught his classes and continued his studies, and was just as unhappy as ever fighting with God to win salvation. Then, in 1510, he was invited to go to the very center of his religion, Rome, and he was sure it was a way to find salvation at last.

The trip was a protest mission against a plan to unify all the Augustinian congregations under a new set of rules. For many years the various Augustinian monasteries had followed different rules. Some had very strict rules, like the monastery at Erfurt; others had more relaxed rules, like the one at Wittenberg. The leaders of the Augustinian order believed that all the monasteries should have the same rules. In 1510 Egidio, the general of the entire Augustinian order, presented a new set of rules and ordered all the monasteries to accept it. He was supported by the pope and by John von Staupitz. But the Erfurt monastery and other strict cloisters thought the new constitution was altogether too weak. They decided to send two representatives to Rome to plead their case. Because the monastery at Erfurt was a large and important one, one of the representatives was chosen from there, and as the monk who followed the monastery's rigid rules to the extreme, Martin Luther was the logical choice. In November 1510 Luther, who was determined to save the strict rules, set out with a monk from a monastery in Nuernberg to walk the 850 miles to Rome.

They walked endlessly, leaving the warm fall weather of the lowlands to climb the snow-covered Alps, trying to plan each day's journey according to the locations of monasteries where they could find shelter for the night. From the wind-swept passes of the Alpine region they descended southward, charting their progress by the ever-larger expanses of rock and green tundra. With every step Luther grew more excited, for he was much more than a representative of his way of life. He was a pilgrim, seeking the peace he was sure he would find in the Eternal City, where the early Christians had died for their beliefs, and where the cardinals and the pope lived and made the major decisions of the church. When, after a journey of more than 40 days, he saw the city, he fell to the ground in thanksgiving. It was the turn of the year, and Luther hoped his visit to Rome would prove to be a turning point in his life. He prayed for a successful mission and for some sign somewhere in the dozens of monasteries and churches that he was worthy of salvation in the eyes of God.

Luther and his companion found shelter in one of the city's 70 monasteries and the very next day went to the Vatican to present their case to General Egidio. Luther secretly hoped the general would not decide on the matter right away, for he wanted time to see the city and visit its shrines. His wish was granted. Egidio and the two monks talked about the matter on and off for four weeks, and when they were not with Egidio, their time was their own.

What struck Luther most about Rome was its sharp contrasts. On the one extreme, there were all the cardinals and church officials in their silk and velvet robes, the shops whose only business was weaving church vestments or baking bread for the Vatican, the shrines with their gold and crystal religious objects. At the other extreme were the thousands of poor Romans living in filth, dressed in rags, weak with hunger. Thieves and pickpockets roamed the streets, orphaned children picked over piles of garbage. The only thing the two groups seemed to have in common was their eagerness to get the tourists' money, and when Martin Luther saw this, he was saddened and hurt.

The priests seemed to be just as greedy as the street people. A priest stood on a corner selling bones that he claimed were the relics of saints, and Luther could not see why that priest was any different from a common peddler. In the churches he was amazed at how fast the priests said masses. The mass had always been very sacred and important to him. Yet these priests seemed to treat the mass the way his father treated the carts of ore from the mines—the faster they moved, the better. And when he told the priests that he was not used to such speed in saying the mass, they laughed at his innocence. Yet he kept on, like all the other tourists, dashing from shrine to church in order to see it all, and did not make any connection between his sense of hurry and that of the priests. He knew only that his visits were not very satisfying. Even amid the hustle and bustle of Rome his doubts returned.

He went to the staircase of Pilate. Christ was supposed to have descended that staircase after being sentenced to death. It was said that by climbing those stairs on his knees one could free the soul of an ancestor from purgatory (that place of temporary banishment where souls were said to be sent to be cleansed of sin before entering heaven). Luther wanted to free his grandfather from purgatory, so he crawled up the stairs, praying and kissing each step. But when he reached the top, he muttered to himself, "Who knows whether it is true?"

After four weeks and many discussions Egidio decided that the strict monasteries should not be allowed to remain separate. Luther and his fellow monk had failed in their mission. But in the end the strict monasteries got their way. Because of continuing opposition the new constitution was never adopted. Even though Luther wished he had been able to get Egidio to change his mind during the visit, he would never regret having seen Rome. "I would not trade my visit to Rome for a hundred thousand gulden," he later said. "If I had not seen it with my own eyes, I would not believe it. Godlessness and evil are so rampant and bold there that no attention is paid to either God or man, to sin or shame." It was a sadder but wiser Martin Luther who set out again for home with his fellow monk.

The two reached Nuernberg at the end of March 1511, and Luther went on alone to Erfurt. There, after making a long report to his superiors about his mission, he returned to his teaching and his studies. But he was not to remain at Erfurt long.

As a highly intelligent man, better educated than most, and as a man who worked so hard for purity, Martin Luther was well respected within the Augustinian order. That is why he had been chosen to go to Rome. On his return he found that he was more respected than ever, even though he had failed in his mission. His position was further strengthened because the vicar general, John von Staupitz, was personally interested in him. Staupitz was not angry with Luther for opposing him on the matter of the new constitution, and at a convention of the Augustinian order at Cologne in the early summer of 1511, Staupitz helped get Luther elected subprior of the monastery at Wittenberg.

Luther moved to Wittenberg not long after that. At age 27 he was one of the youngest subpriors ever to serve at the monastery, and his election was due not just to Staupitz' influence but to Luther's own ability. Still, there remained a broad streak of immaturity in the promising young monk. He was still so taken up with his battle for salvation that Staupitz did not know what to do about him. He had tried pointing out different ways to view God the Father and Christ, but that had not worked. He had tried advising Luther to relax and give in to the idea of God's love, but that had not worked either. One day he cried in exasperation, "I don't understand it!" Luther was really surprised at this. He asked Staupitz if he had not felt the same doubts. Certainly he had felt doubt and despair, said Staupitz, but not like Luther. "I think they are your meat and drink," he said, hinting at his belief that Luther somehow enjoyed torturing himself. But sarcasm did not work any better than the other tactics. Finally Staupitz decided that the only way to save Luther from himself was to give him so much to do he would not have time for himself.

One day in the garden of the Wittenberg cloister, as the two stood in the shade of a pear tree, Staupitz told Luther that he wanted him to become a preacher and to study for his doctor's degree so he could become a regular professor at the university. Luther was shocked: preach and study for the doctor's degree too? The work load would kill him!

"Quite all right," said Staupitz dryly. "God has plenty of work for clever men to do in heaven."

Unable to persuade Staupitz that he could not do what had been asked of him, Luther was forced to agree. He began studying toward the degree of Doctor of Theology. He was used to studying and enjoyed it, so that part was not hard. Preaching was another matter. He enjoyed teaching, but as a preacher he would not be talking to a small class of students but to the ordinary people of Wittenberg; he did not know how to talk to people in the outside world.

He worked hard on his first sermon. When he decided he could do no more with it, he presented it to the other monks in the monastery dining room. They liked it, so he took it to the people. At certain scheduled times the people of the town came to an old wooden chapel on the monastery grounds to hear sermons given by the monks. The small audiences who heard Luther preach seemed to like his sermons, which painted a less stern God than the one who tormented Luther. He had no desire to teach others the images of God the Father and Christ he had learned, so he softened those images as much as he could. Before long the prior of the Wittenberg

Dr. Martin Luther as the serious professor and scholar in academic attire with robe and beret. Luther obtained the degree, doctor of theology, on Oct. 19, 1512, from the University of Wittenberg. Painting by Lucas Cranach the Elder, 1528. (Kunstsammlungen zu Weimar)

cloister appointed him the official monastery preacher.

As the monastery preacher, Luther traveled to the altars around Wittenberg and preached his sermons there. He visited the sick, heard confession, comforted those who were troubled, and answered the letters requesting help that daily arrived at the monastery. There were so many letters that they alone took up a lot of time, and he complained that he could certainly use a couple of secretaries. But John von Staupitz just laughed at Luther's complaints. He wanted Luther to be so busy helping others that he would be too tired to worry about himself.

Meanwhile Luther studied, and by the fall of 1512 he had passed all the tests for the Doctor of Theology degree. In October a ceremony was held in the Castle Church in Wittenberg. As Luther's fellow students looked on, Professor Andreas Carlstadt placed the doctor's ring on Luther's finger and presented him with the highest degree a student of theology could earn. After the official ceremony ended, the other students crowded around Luther, lifted him up on their shoulders, and paraded him through the streets of the town. Riding on the crest of the human wave beneath him, Luther felt a deep gratitude to John von Staupitz. If it had not been for the older man's belief in him and challenge to him, he would never have become Doctor Martin Luther.

Staupitz was not finished with Luther. In fact, his challenge to the younger man was just beginning. Almost as soon as Luther received his degree, Staupitz retired from his chair at Wittenberg University, as professor of the Bible. Martin Luther was named to take his place and became the youngest member of the theological faculty. It is not known if Staupitz retired so that Luther could take his place, but it was certainly good timing. As a professor of the Bible, Luther would be forced to study that book, study it intensely. Deep study of the Bible was not necessary in many branches of religious education. If Luther had continued to teach, say, moral philosophy, he would have needed only a small amount of Bible study. But John von Staupitz wanted Luther to study the Bible. He believed it was the only way Luther would find inner peace. Staupitz would prove to be right, but the very study that would end Luther's inner turmoil would also bring about the end of his friendship with the man who had done the most for him.

Chapter VI.
LUTHER DISCOVERS THE GOSPEL OF GOD

Martin Luther wanted to be good at his new job, so he decided to learn the Bible inside and out. That meant studying the Bible not just in its Latin translation but in the languages in which it had been written first—Hebrew and Greek. To do that, he had to learn Hebrew and Greek. He worked in his private office on the second floor of a monastery tower, burning candle after candle as he tried to understand the Scriptures. He found that he really enjoyed studying the Bible, and he shared that enjoyment with his students and with the common people of Wittenberg when he preached his sermons. He was still the official preacher of the monastery at Wittenberg, and the more he studied the Bible, the more he included what he had learned in his sermons. Many of the common people had never seen a Bible, and as word got around that Dr. Luther was talking about what was written in it, more people came to the monastery to hear him. After awhile the small chapel on the monastery grounds could not hold the crowds, and in 1514 Luther started preaching in the larger St. Mary's Church in town.

The more he studied the Bible, the more hopeful Martin Luther began to feel. Through his reading of the Psalms he began to see Christ in a new light and came to understand that He did not enjoy condemning sinners at all but suffered with them. He also began to view God in a different way and to appreciate the love God must have for man; after all, He had sent His own Son to die for man's sins. But it was while studying Paul's Epistle (Letter) to the Romans that Martin Luther had a true revelation and found peace at last.

53

It probably happened sometime in 1514. As usual, Luther was working in his private office in the monastery tower. He was studying longer and burning more candles than usual because he was very much interested in Paul's letter and in Paul himself. Paul was a Jew and a Roman citizen who grew up hating Christians. In fact, he helped to persecute the early Christians.

One day, while he was traveling to Damascus to arrest any Christians he found there, Paul suddenly saw a light so blinding that he fell to the ground.

Then he heard a voice say, "Paul, Paul, why are you persecuting Me?"

"Who are You, Lord?" Paul asked in amazement.

"I am Jesus," the voice answered, "and you are persecuting Me."

Paul did an about-face on religion after that. He became a strong defender of the Christians and helped to spread the Christian Gospel, or Good News. In the beginning he had some trouble understanding why Christ had come to earth, and he was confused between the image of God he had been taught and the image of God that Christ wanted him to see. At last, he had come to understand.

Since Martin Luther was having the same problem that Paul had, he studied this part of the Bible very closely. Over and over he read verses 16 and 17 of the first chapter of Paul's epistle: "I am not ashamed of the Gospel: It is the power of God for salvation to everyone who has faith. . . . For in it the righteousness of God is revealed through faith for faith, as it is written: 'The righteous shall live by faith.' "

Paul seemed to be saying that the idea of God's righteousness was a comforting idea. Martin could not understand that at all. God's righteousness had always seemed to Martin to be a terrible thing. Puzzled, he turned to his Greek dictionaries, and there he discovered that there were many different meanings in Greek for the word that was translated as "righteousness" in Latin. One of the meanings of the Greek word was *mercy!*

Luther thought about other places where the term "righteousness of God" appeared in the Scriptures. He grew very excited as he realized that in these places, too, it could mean "the work of God" or "the power of God" or "the wisdom of God" or "the glory of God." When translated in these ways,

54

it was a wonderful term, not a harsh and frightening one. Luther would say later, "Here I felt that I was altogether born anew and had entered Paradise itself through open gates."

Now Luther could understand the God who had sent His own Son to die for man's sins. He could understand the idea that God was loving and merciful. It was right there in the Scriptures. After struggling for nearly 10 years to win salvation, Luther found out at last that all he needed was to have faith in Christ. He had found his "gracious God." A remarkable change came over him. He put on weight and his eyes lost that haunted look that had made him look so much older than he was. He stopped punishing himself because he realized that was not what God wanted at all.

Martin Luther shared his happy discovery with his students and with the people who came to hear his sermons. As time went on, he was in great demand as a speaker and lecturer. Meanwhile he continued to study the Scriptures and grew troubled as he found more and more differences between the Bible and the practices and teachings of the church. He found that certain well-known legends about the apostles had absolutely no basis in the New Testament. And the way the church taught people to worship the saints seemed to Luther to be too extreme and not at all in keeping with Christ's simple teachings. Luther also went back to the writings of St. Augustine and found, to his surprise, that Augustine's teachings had been forgotten or ignored too. Most of the professors at the University of Wittenberg were members of the Augustinian order, but the things they taught were not like the teachings of St. Augustine at all.

Luther was no revolutionary, but he believed it was wrong for the church to have gotten so far away from the Bible and for the Augustinian order to know so little about the teachings of its founder. He hoped to bring about change in these matters. He hoped to educate his students to read and use the Bible and the writings of St. Augustine and to place more importance on them than on church decrees and doctrines. To do so, he began assigning his students to read the Bible and began giving more lectures on St. Augustine's teachings. Word of what Luther was doing got around the university, and more students started coming to his classes. The other professors of religion were not at all happy about this. In fact, they wanted him to stop teaching these new ideas. They might have been able to stop him if Andreas Carlstadt had not come over to Luther's side.

Carlstadt had been a professor at the university since it opened and was dean of the faculty. He had received Luther's doctoral oath and placed the doctor's cap on Luther's head. He respected the younger man's intelligence and did not believe that Luther would deliberately misquote the teachings of St.

Andreas Bodenstein, also called Carlstadt, an iconoclast. And old engraving by an unknown artist. (Lutherhalle, Wittenberg)

An original letter of indulgence, dated 1488. (Archiv und Bibliothek, Evangelisches Ministerium, Erfurt)

Augustine. Carlstadt had never studied Augustine's writings, but if he had been a different sort of man, he would have pretended he had. After all, Luther was challenging his own teachings. Instead Carlstadt was willing to learn. He went to Leipzig to buy an edition of the works of St. Augustine. He studied the material thoroughly and realized that Luther was right. With someone as important as Carlstadt on his side, Luther had little trouble from then on. Many professors still did not believe what he was teaching, but they made no move against him.

The citizens of Wittenberg did not care very much about the controversy that was going on at the university. But they did care about the next cause Luther took up. They were surprised and troubled when he began to tell them not to put their faith in indulgences as a form of penance.

Penance was a way of paying for one's sins, so it would not be necessary to spend a lot of time in purgatory after death. Souls who had sinned a lot and not done penance on earth could spend an eternity there.

People could do penance in two basic ways. First, they could confess their sins to a priest who would order them to say prayers or to do good works to prove they were sorry. That is how poor people did penance. More well-to-do people could take a shortcut. Instead of doing good works, they could donate money to the church and receive an indulgence, a sort of promise that the punishment for their sins would not be harsh. The promise was given in the form of a letter signed by the pope.

The pope was actually responsible for all indulgences because he was at the head of the church. But he could name representatives to sell indulgences for him. Frederick the Wise, the elector of Saxony, had been granted that right by the pope. Frederick had a huge collection of relics of various saints. This all started when he inherited what was said to be a genuine thorn from the crown of Christ. He then decided to collect more relics and journeyed to all parts of Europe to do so. By 1509 he had gathered 5,005 relics, and by 1520 his collection would number 19,013 pieces. They included a variety of relics of Christ: a piece of His swaddling clothes, 13 pieces of His crib, a wisp of straw, one piece of gold and three pieces of myrrh brought by the three Wise Men, a strand of hair from His beard, one of the nails driven into His hands at the crucifixion, a piece of the bread served at the Last Supper, and a piece of the stone on which Jesus had stood as He ascended to heaven after His resurrection. Other items in Frederick's collection included bones of various saints, pieces of their clothing, hair from their heads, teeth, and a variety of other relics. All these were certified by the church as genuine. Frederick the Wise knew he could never collect as many relics as Rome had, but he made every effort to make Wittenberg the "Rome of Germany."

Frederick opened his collection to the public once each year, on November 1, or All Saints' Day. On this day people came to look at the relics and to buy the indulgences attached to them. Money from the sale of indulgences had paid for the building of both Wittenberg University and the Wittenberg cloister, and every November 1 Frederick the Wise collected more money to continue his plans for his town.

Martin Luther had bought indulgences. He understood that the sale of indulgences was a way for the church to raise money and that both where he taught and where he lived had been paid for in this way. What bothered him was that the people who bought them thought they were buying forgiveness from God. Luther knew that indulgences were originally meant only to release a person from the penance ordered by the *church*. Even the church could not speak for God.

Pope Leo X, who decreed the sale of indulgences for the construction of St. Peter's in Rome. Woodcut by an unknown artist, 16th century. (Lutherhalle, Wittenberg)

Luther's parishioners believed that by paying a sum of money and getting a letter signed by the pope they could buy God's forgiveness. This bothered him a lot. He wanted them to ask God Himself for forgiveness, and in 1516 he preached three sermons against putting too much faith in indulgences. "True inner sorrow and repentance for sin is much more important than buying indulgences," he explained. He gave the third sermon on Halloween, the evening before All Saints' Day, the date of Frederick's annual indulgence sale. This did not please the elector, but he took no formal action against Luther.

Luther in turn was not looking for a fight. He did not want to ruin Frederick's annual sale; nor did he wish to embarrass the church by criticizing this practice. But he cared about his parishioners, and thanks to his old friend and adviser John von Staupitz he had a great number of parishioners to care about. In 1515 Staupitz had appointed Luther district vicar of the Augustinians with responsibility for 11 cloisters.

In 1516 Martin Luther turned 33. He didn't fast too long or physically punish himself anymore, so he had gained back some of the weight he had lost. His cheeks were no longer sunken, his eyes no longer haunted-looking. His high cheekbones and square jaw gave his face a look of strength, and his eyes, dark and bright as ever, were filled with the quiet knowing that simple faith in Christ as his Savior was all he needed to be saved. The doubts and hopelessness of his youth had given way to a sense of peace and calm. He still had great energy, but he no longer used it up doing battle with God and with himself. He used it instead to help other people. At another time in history Martin Luther might have lived the rest of his life quietly, gradually rising to higher positions of authority in the Augustinian order and in the university. But in Germany in the early part of the 16th century events were taking place that a man like Martin Luther could not ignore, even if getting involved in them meant giving up his new-found peace of mind.

Chapter VII.
THE 95 THESES

All his life Luther had never done things halfway. When he'd thought he could win salvation by punishing himself, he'd half killed himself. When he'd found that many church teachings were different from the Bible, he had thrown himself into the study of the Bible. Now he was convinced that the things most people believed about God and religion were wrong, and he wanted them changed, and the sooner the better. His tower revelation may have brought him inner peace, but it had not brought him patience.

Still, he never expected to start a national controversy. But this is just what happened when indulgences began to be misused in a way that Luther could not agree with.

It all started when the Brandenburgs, a family of nobles, decided to try to take control of the church in Germany by getting 23-year-old Albert of Brandenburg appointed to three high offices in the church. This was not exactly legal, but the Brandenburgs knew that money talked louder than principle. Pope Leo needed money to finish building the new St. Peter's Church in Rome and was willing to let Albert have all three offices for the right amount of money.

The Brandenburgs did not have enough money, so they borrowed it from the Fuggers, a wealthy German lending house. In return Pope Leo said they could sell indulgences so they could pay back the loan to the Fuggers. He also wanted half the proceeds from the indulgence sale on top of the money already paid him. And so the bargain was struck.

In 1517 Albert asked John Tetzel, a Dominican monk from Leipzig, who was known as an excellent salesman, to run the sale of the indulgences. Albert then gave Tetzel a list of instructions as to how the indulgences should be advertised, and these instructions went far beyond the promises usually given when indulgences were sold. Tetzel was to tell

MDXX III
SIC·OCVLOS·SIC·ILLE·GENAS·SIC·ORA·FEREBAT·
ANNO·ETATIS·SVE·XXXIIII

ALBERTVS·MI·DI·SA·SANG·ROMANAE·ECCLAE·TI·SAN·
CHRYSOGONI·PBR·CARDINA·MAGVN·AC·MAGDE·
ARC·HIEPS·ELECTOR·IMPE·PRIMAS·ADMNI·
HALBER·MARCHI·BRANDENBVRGENSIS·

Cardinal Albert of Brandenburg, archbishop of
Magdeburg, archbishop and administrator of
Halberstadt, and electoral prince of Mainz. En-
graving by Albrecht Duerer, 1519. (Lutherhalle,
Wittenberg)

people they could buy release from *all* penalties, whether
ordered by the church *or by God*, even for one's relatives in
purgatory. Needless to say, Tetzel immediately began to do a
lot of business.

Frederick the Wise would not allow Tetzel into Saxony.
He did not want money from his territory to go to the power-
hungry Brandenburgs. Besides, he did not want competition
against his own annual indulgence sale. But the border of
Saxony was only 20 miles away from Wittenberg, and people
were willing to make the journey once word got around about
what kind of indulgences Tetzel was offering.

It is not known how much Luther knew about the
political and financial dealings that led up to the Tetzel
indulgence sale, but what he did know was enough to enrage
him. People in his pastorate began coming to confession with

letters they had gotten from Tetzel after they had bought indulgences—letters that forgave them every sin imaginable. They seemed to think they were freed forever from all guilt and didn't have to worry anymore about seeking God's forgiveness. Luther refused to honor the letters, and the parishioners angrily returned to Tetzel to get their money back. This made Tetzel angry, and he started attacking Luther.

Then, somehow, Luther managed to get a copy of Albert's instructions to his salesmen, and what he read enraged him even more. No one, not even the pope, had the power to grant such sweeping pardons! He sat down and wrote out arguments against each point in Albert's instructions, and when he finished, he had a total of 95 statements, or theses.

The Dominican monk John Tetzel, as an indulgence salesman. Engraving by J. J. Vogel, 1727. (Lutherhalle, Wittenberg)

In the theses Luther said that the poor were being cheated out of money that was better spent caring for their families. He said that money spent on indulgences by richer people should instead be spent on charity. He admitted that the pope had the right to grant indulgences and pardons for penalties *he* had ordered, but the pope could not erase punishments ordered by God and so could not release souls from purgatory. He declared that the living could have God's forgiveness by being sorry for their sins and needed no indulgences. In fact, as long as they put their faith in indulgences, they could not hope to win salvation. He called these statements *Ninety-Five Theses on the Power and Efficacy of Indulgences.*

In those days, if a scholar wanted to debate on a subject, he wrote out his arguments, or theses, in Latin and posted them in a public place. This is what Luther did. First, he had his theses printed up and sent copies to Albert of Brandenburg and others who were involved, with letters telling what Tetzel was doing and urging that he be stopped. Then, on October 31, 1517, the eve of All Saints' Day, Luther took a hammer and nails and a copy of the *95 Theses* and posted them on the door of the Castle Church at Wittenberg.

The timing was no accident. John Tetzel had left the area by then, but the very next day the annual indulgence sale of Frederick the Wise would take place, and Luther had decided it was high time the whole issue of indulgences was debated, no matter how the elector felt about it. Still, Luther didn't expect a public controversy. He had written the theses in Latin, not in German. He thought the debate would take place within the world of the university and the church.

No one came to debate the theses in person. No one sent any written arguments. No word came from Albert of Brandenburg or from any of the others to whom Luther had sent copies of his theses. For a full two weeks after Luther nailed the theses to the church door, an almost eerie silence seemed to surround them, like the calm before a storm. Then the storm struck.

By the end of the two weeks word began to reach Luther that his theses were being read by many scholars and churchmen. Not much later he learned that they were being translated into German. From letters and documents we know that the theses were being talked about in Merseburg, Hamburg, Nuernberg, Lochau, and Dresden. Some people agreed with them, others violently disagreed, but no one who either heard about or saw the theses ignored them.

When Albert received Luther's letter and the copy of the theses, he sent an official protest against Luther to Rome.

Printed copy of Luther's 95 Theses in Latin. (Lutherhalle, Wittenberg)

John Tetzel did not remain quiet either. In January 1518 the German Dominicans met at Frankfurt, and Tetzel read 106 theses against Luther. The Dominicans also decided to complain to Rome. In response the Augustinians held their own meeting at Heidelberg. They decided that the matter could be cleared up if Luther just wrote some more theses to explain the first 95.

Meanwhile most ordinary Germans, who could not read, did not know much about the controversy. But they sensed that the power of the church was somehow being challenged, and most were pleased about that. Like Luther's father, they depended on the church but resented it deeply.

All this time Rome was surprisingly quiet. At first Pope Leo did not take the matter seriously. It was reported that when he learned of the theses he called Luther a drunken German who would think differently when he sobered up. Later, when the news from Germany showed that a wide-spread controversy was raging, Leo X still did not take action. He thought the Germans could deal with the problem. He probably saw it all as a tempest in a teapot and did not think it would affect him. But when Luther's attackers began to call him a traitor against the church and to beg Rome to do something about the man, the pope's advisers decided they had to act. *No one* was supposed to criticize the church and get away with it. In June 1518 a summons was issued ordering Luther to appear in Rome in 60 days. Luther received the summons on August 7.

Luther was afraid that if he left Germany he would never return. He knew of many men who had been burned at the stake for attacking church practices. So he went to Frederick the Wise for help. Frederick did not agree with Luther's ideas. At the same time he did not want the man to be denied a fair hearing, and he felt that this was exactly what might happen. At that time a diet, or congress, was being held in the city of Augsburg. Cardinal Cajetan, general of the German Dominicans, was there representing the pope, and Frederick decided to contact him. Would Cajetan be willing to hold a hearing for Luther in Germany? Cajetan agreed, and in early October Luther set off for Augsburg to be interviewed by the cardinal. Luther was glad he did not have to go to Rome, but he did not expect to get a fair hearing at Augsburg. After all, Cajetan was a Dominican, just like John Tetzel, the indul-

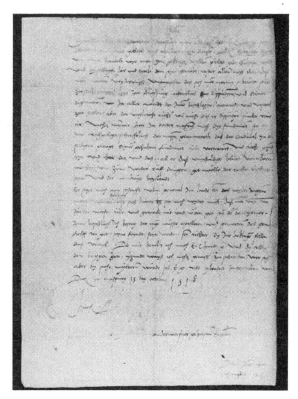

An original letter by John Staupitz to the elector of Saxony, Frederick the Wise, in which Staupitz reports on Luther's conference with Cardinal Cajetan in Augsburg, 1518. The letter is dated Oct. 15, 1518. (Archiv und Bibliothek, Erfurt)

gence salesman. As he started for Augsburg, he said to himself, "Now I must die. What a disgrace I shall be to my parents!"

Luther and Cajetan had three interviews in Augsburg in the middle of October. Luther's old friend and adviser, John von Staupitz, was present as Cardinal Cajetan questioned Luther about his theories and tried to prove him wrong. But Luther was an excellent debater. Although he was probably shaking with fear inside, he was not about to take back the things he had said and written. In fact, he was downright rude to Cajetan. The angry cardinal ordered him out of his sight and warned him not to return unless he was ready to apologize. Luther would not apologize. It was a stalemate situation.

Staupitz realized he could do nothing. Sadly he left Augsburg. Before he left, he released Luther from his vow of obedience to the Augustinian order, because he realized that in such a time of crisis Luther might not be able to keep that vow. Luther felt as if his friend had deserted him. The two would never be close again.

Luther waited around for a week to see whether Cajetan would call him in for another interview, but nothing happened. Meanwhile Luther's friends in Augsburg heard rumors that he would be arrested, and they were very much worried. Finally they could take the suspense no longer. One night they woke Luther up and hustled him to a waiting horse. He should have had breeches, spurs, and stirrups for riding, but there was no time for that. In the dead of night, with his monk's cowl flapping in the wind behind him, Martin Luther fled Augsburg. He arrived back in Wittenberg one day shy of a year after he had nailed his *95 Theses* to the door of the Castle Church. In that year he had risen from an almost unknown monk to become a man whose name was known throughout Germany; and now he was a fugitive. He couldn't believe how much had happened just because he had tried to get a scholarly debate going on indulgences.

When Cardinal Cajetan learned that Luther was back in Wittenberg, he wrote Frederick the Wise demanding that he either send Luther to Rome or banish him from his territories. Frederick did not know what to do. He knew the pope was angry with Luther, and Frederick, a devout Catholic, certainly did not want to go against the pope. On the other hand, Leo had not actually said Luther was a heretic, or a church traitor. Frederick did not want to jump the gun. He decided not to obey Cajetan's order.

A less powerful man would not have been able to get away with disobeying Cajetan. Frederick, one of the seven electors, was indeed powerful, and at the end of 1518 he was in an important political position. Maximilian, emperor of the Holy Roman Empire of the German Nation, was very old and close to death. A successor would soon be named, and Frederick the Wise was a possible candidate.

The way things were, Pope Leo did not want to put pressure on Frederick. So he sent a German named Charles von Miltitz to visit Frederick and try to work out a compromise. At the inns where Miltitz stopped on his way to

Wittenberg, he questioned the people and found that three of every four were against the pope and for Luther. He declared that no case had been so troublesome to the church in a thousand years and that Rome would gladly pay 10,000 ducats to be rid of it.

Neither Frederick nor Luther was going to take any bribes. Miltitz begged Luther to take back what he had said and written. Luther refused. Miltitz asked that he at least stay away from further controversy. Luther said he would not be silent in the face of attack. What if his attackers stopped? Miltitz asked. In that case, Luther said, he would agree to be silent. Miltitz' report back to Rome caused the pope and his advisers to believe that the Luther problem was practically solved.

But in no time at all the silence was broken. For months now, Professor John Eck of the University of Ingolstadt had been writing pamphlets against Luther. Andreas Carlstadt, dean of the faculty at Wittenberg, who had gone over to

Dr. John Eck, professor of theology at the University of Ingolstadt. He debated with Luther in Leipzig in 1519 and forced Luther to admit that the Roman Church may have erred when it convicted John Huss in 1415. Engraving by an unknown artist, 1735. (Lutherhalle, Wittenberg)

St. Thomas Church in Leipzig. Present-day view from the east. The ceremonies for the famous religious debate between Eck and Luther began here in 1519. George Rhau, then the choir master of the now famous *Thomanerchor*, composed a special mass for the occasion.

Luther's side when he first started questioning the university's religious teachings, started answering those writings with pamphlets of his own. In the spring of 1519 Eck challenged Carlstadt to a public debate at the University of Leipzig. Luther did not like the idea of another man speaking for him. He felt he had to go to the debate too, even if it meant breaking his silence. The debate was set for late June 1519.

In that month Frederick the Wise voted for Maximilian's grandson, Charles V of Spain, as the new emperor of the Holy Roman Empire of the German Nation. Charles was elected unanimously, and with his election Germany was brought under the same ruler as the huge and powerful Spanish empire. But there were many political questions and problems to be dealt with now that Charles V had been elected. And since Charles was too busy with the affairs of Spain to pay much attention to Germany for awhile, Frederick remained an important figure. Rome was still

Philipp Melanchthon, who primarily drafted the *Confessio Augustana* to be presented at the Diet of Augsburg in 1530. Painting by Lucas Cranach the Younger, 1537. (Staatliche Kunsthalle, Karlsruhe)

afraid to push him on the Luther case.

The debate at Leipzig began on June 27, 1519. Feelings on both sides were running so high that Luther, Carlstadt, and Philip Melanchthon, a young professor of Greek who strongly supported Luther, arrived with 200 students armed with battle-axes, and Eck had a bodyguard of 76 men provided by the Leipzig town council. So many people came to the debate that no hall in the university was large enough to hold them all, and the debate was moved to the auditorium of Leipzig Castle. Certainly the matters to be debated were of great interest to the people, but it is likely that many went to Leipzig just to see Martin Luther.

The *95 Theses* and later writings of Luther had been translated and widely published. John Froben, a printer friend in Basel, had collected all these writings in a single edition and in February 1519 reported to Luther that he was nearly sold out. Six hundred copies had been sent to France and Spain, and orders had come in from England and Switzerland. Copies were even being circulated secretly in Rome. Luther was fast becoming an international celebrity.

An eyewitness to the debate described Luther: "Martin is of middle height, emaciated from care and study, so that you can almost count his bones through the skin. He is in the vigor of manhood and has a clear, penetrating voice. He is learned and has the Scripture at his fingers' ends. He knows Greek and Hebrew sufficiently to judge of the interpretations. A perfect forest of words and ideas stands at his command. He is affable and friendly, in no sense dour or arrogant. He is equal to anything. In company he is vivacious, jocose, always cheerful and gay no matter how hard his adversaries press him. Everyone chides him for the fault of being a little too insolent in his reproaches and more caustic than is prudent for an innovator in religion or becoming to a theologian."

For the first few days of the debate Luther was not heard except "in company." The debate was between Eck and Carlstadt. It was hard for Luther simply to watch what was going on, because Eck was a better speaker and much more of a crowd pleaser than Carlstadt. Then, on July 14, 1519, Luther took up the debate with Eck, and their battle of words went on for 10 days. There was hardly any debate on indulgences, over which the trouble had first started. Since October 31, 1517, the church had taken steps to stop the worst indulgence practices, and Eck agreed with those reforms. Luther later said that if he had been answered with the views of Eck on indulgences when he first posted the *95 Theses*, "the world would have never heard of Martin Luther." The debate centered instead on the church and the office of the pope: whether the pope governed by divine right or by human right. Pushed by Eck, Luther was forced to go beyond what he had intended to say and to state that no man or institution was infallible (could not be wrong). The only thing that was infallible was the revealed Word of God, the Scriptures. Such statements were pure heresy or false teaching in the eyes of Rome.

The debate ended not because Eck and Luther had run out of things to say but because the castle auditorium was needed for the entertainment of a visiting nobleman. The records of the debate were sent to the universities of Erfurt and Paris for a decision on the winner (Paris never reported back at all, Erfurt not for two years). John Eck went almost directly to Rome to report to the pope and his advisers. Luther returned to Wittenberg, aware that he would probably hear from Rome soon.

Luther found it hard to believe that he could have gotten himself into so much trouble when all he had meant to do was start a movement to bring about needed changes. Back in 1517 he had never expected to state in public that the pope was not infallible. Yet all the thought and study he had put into defending his views had led him to that conclusion, and he could not keep silent about it. Many times he wondered if he was wrong, but each time he carefully weighed the facts as he saw them, and the answer was the same.

During the debate Eck had demanded, "Are you the only one who knows anything?"

Luther had replied, "I will tell you straight what I think. I am a Christian theologian; and I am bound, not only to assert, but to defend the truth with my blood and death. I want to believe freely and be a slave to the authority of no one, whether council, university, or pope. I will confidently confess what appears to me to be true, whether it has been asserted by a Catholic or a heretic, whether it has been approved or reproved by a council."

For defending the truth as he saw it, Luther expected to lose his life.

Chapter VIII.
THE EXCOMMUNICATION OF MARTIN LUTHER

The next few months were very busy for Martin Luther. He knew it was only a matter of time before Rome took action against him, and he had much to do. He was still teaching; in fact he had more students than he knew what to do with. They came streaming in from all over Germany and included learned scholars as well as young men just starting their education. Almost single-handedly he had put the small and struggling University of Wittenberg on the map.

He still had his duties as a pastor and a monk. He did not *have* to perform them anymore, because John von Staupitz had released him from his vows at Erfurt. But he chose to do them anyway. All the while he was studying and writing. He was beyond the point of no return. He was in so much trouble that he believed he could never get out of it, and so he was determined to have his say. He was racing against time. Before long, he knew, he would have to give up some of his duties or collapse from exhaustion.

What he gave up were his official prayers. With so much to do, he often did not have time to say the number of prayers he was supposed to say each day. So he would keep track of the prayers he "owed" for two or three weeks and then would take a whole day off to repay his "debt" of prayer. Once he found himself with such a huge debt that he prayed for three whole days without food or drink or sleep and became so physically and mentally exhausted that he could not sleep even when he tried. For five days he lay in bed, but he was unable to sleep until a doctor gave him a sleeping potion. It was days more before he felt normal again. Afterward, like a person who has eaten so much food that he can't stand the sight of it, Luther could not bear even to look at his prayerbook. He went for three months without saying the official prayers, and faced with the fact that the debt was too large to repay, he gave up. From then on he still prayed but no longer kept track of the prayers he "owed" and the prayers he had "paid."

Luther wrote and published three important pamphlets during 1520. In one he said that people should be priests to one another and that everyone who was baptized should spread the good news that through faith in Jesus Christ our sins are forgiven. At the same time he said there should still be regular priests, so he wasn't really going against the church with this idea.

In another pamphlet, and in the letter that went along with it, he seemed to try to make peace with Pope Leo. He said he was not attacking Leo personally but rather the false teachings that Leo was not trying to stop. Luther's followers were surprised and disappointed at this. They accused him of "copping out," as we would put it today. But that is not what he was doing. Yet it would be hard to blame him if he had been. He was frightened. He did not want to be burned at the stake. He was only a man, and there were times when he wondered if he was doing the right thing in the right way, when he felt completely out of touch with God, when he lay awake nights shivering in terror, when he would have done anything to escape what seemed like purgatory on earth. Anything? Anything except take back the truths he had learned from Holy Scripture. This, he told the pope, he could not do.

The third pamphlet was obviously written when he was feeling very brave. More than anything he had said or written before, this pamphlet was almost guaranteed to send him to the fiery stake.

The church taught that Christ had started seven sacraments: Baptism, confirmation, the Lord's Supper, marriage, the ordination of priests, penance, and extreme unction (oil put on a person's body at death). Luther announced that he

75

had studied the Scriptures and found that most of the seven were *man's* inventions, not Christ's. He said that confirmation, marriage, ordination, and extreme unction were not sacraments because there was nothing in the Scriptures to show that Christ had anything to do with starting them. Christ *had* made Baptism a sacrament by saying: "Baptizing them in the name of the Father and of the Son and of the Holy Ghost." And: "He who believes and is baptized will be saved." Christ *had* shared bread and wine with His disciples, declaring the bread to be His body and the wine to be His blood, telling them: "Do this." So the Lord's Supper, or Holy Communion, was a real sacrament. Finally, Christ *had* forgiven people who were sorry for their sins, so penance (being sorry, confessing, and being forgiven) was also a sort of half-sacrament, not on the same level as Baptism and the Lord's Supper. The rest, except marriage, were just man's inventions and not sacraments at all.

This was a truly revolutionary set of ideas. Even some of Luther's strong supporters were amazed and worried when they read the pamphlet. Once Pope Leo and his advisers saw this, there could be no hope for Martin Luther. But as it turned out, this pamphlet had nothing to do with what Rome decided. The pope acted before he saw any of the pamphlets.

On June 15, 1520, Leo X put his signature to a papal bull, or document, that charged Luther with being a traitor against the church, ordered all his works burned, and called for him to be excommunicated (outlawed) from the church unless, within 60 days after he received the bull, he took back everything he had written or said.

Luther did not receive the bull until October 10, four months later. He had been visiting printers in a variety of cities, and the bull followed him throughout Germany before it reached him. By the time he did get it, the burning of his writings had already started. The first bonfire was lit in a public square in Rome while the bull was still being printed, and throughout the summer and early fall there were other bonfires in cities across the German empire.

In the cities where most everyone was against Luther, the representatives of the pope had little trouble burning his works. But in the cities where Luther had a lot of friends, these representatives had a dangerous mission. Professor John Eck, who had debated with Luther and Carlstadt at

Leipzig, was put in charge of the eastern sections of the empire. At Leipzig itself he had to go to a cloister to hide from an angry mob. At Erfurt students called the bull a "bulloon" and threw all the copies into the river. At Torgau the bull was torn down from where it was posted and was smeared with dirt. In other cities mobs tried to put out the fires that were destroying Luther's books.

On December 10, 1520, Martin Luther held a bonfire of his own. The date marked the 60th day after he had received the papal bull. He had not taken back any of his writings during that time, and he decided to mark the end of the period of grace in his own way. He asked his friend and colleague Philip Melanchthon to invite the students and faculty to meet at the east gate of the city at 10 o'clock in the morning. Then he asked that a fire be laid at the site. Hundreds of people showed up, and at Luther's signal the fire was lit. "Since they burned my books, I burn theirs," he announced, and into the fire he threw a pamphlet that attacked his teachings. The students and professors did the same, throwing into the fire all writings that supported the teachings of Rome. As the fire consumed them, Luther threw in the volumes of the Canon Law, the most sacred writings of the church. Then he pulled the papal bull out of his pocket and threw that into the fire too.

Everyone cheered and sang. Then the professors went home. But the students were too excited to leave. They paraded through the streets, singing and shouting. The people of Wittenberg cheered them as they passed. The students were still celebrating the next day, when the town authorities finally stopped them.

Luther did not join the students. As the fire died down, so did his happiness and excitement. The 60 days were up, and he had an idea that it wouldn't be long before he was formally excommunicated. He was right. Rome took action—very quickly, for Rome. Martin Luther was excommunicated from the Catholic Church on January 3, 1521. Since there was no other church in Europe, he was a man without a church, and that was like being a man without a country.

But the case was far from over. According to German law no German of any rank could be taken out of Germany for trial, and no one should be outlawed without a hearing. When the new emperor, Charles V of Spain, finally arrived in Germany to be crowned as Holy Roman Emperor in Novem-

Emperor Charles V as a young man. When the emperor sat before Luther on April 17, 1521, Charles V, on whose realm the sun did not set, was only 21 years old. Woodcut by Albrecht Duerer. (Lutherhalle, Wittenberg)

ber 1520, he found that he would have to deal with that law and with the Luther case.

The 20-year-old Charles had no idea how big the Luther controversy was. When he got to Germany, he was amazed at how high feelings ran on all sides. The Diet (Congress) of Worms, which he opened when he got to that German city, was so taken up by arguments for and against Luther that Charles realized no other business would get done unless the case was settled.

Charles ordered Luther to be invited to appear before the diet in April 1521. He was invited to answer the pope's bull, not argue about it. If he agreed to take back his criticisms of the church, it might be possible to get the pope to lift the ban on him. If Luther refused, the diet would support the ban, but at least it would have given him a hearing.

Luther accepted the invitation, but he was tired of hearings and interviews. He had no intention of taking back the things he'd said and written, so he knew what the diet would decide.

Charles V promised that Luther would have safe conduct on his journey to Worms, but Luther realized this was no guarantee that he would ever reach Worms alive. There were rumors that he would be attacked on the way and that the pope's supporters would try to kidnap him and take him to Rome for trial. At the last minute even George Spalatin, Luther's friend and the court preacher to Frederick the Wise, warned him not to go to Worms, but Luther's mind was made up. A great sense of peace had come over him. He had prayed over his trouble and was sure once again that he was speaking for Christ and doing the right thing. If he had to die for his beliefs, he was ready.

Casper Sturm, imperial herald to Charles V, arrived in Wittenberg in late March 1521 with the letter of safe conduct. On April 2 Luther's small party set out to make the 300-mile journey to Worms. In the lead was Sturm on horseback, carrying the imperial banner with its black, two-headed eagle and the royal coat of arms on a yellow silk background. Behind him Luther rode in a two-wheeled, horse-drawn cart with three friends, who kept looking from side to side as if they expected an ambush at any moment. Luther took out his lute and began to strum it and sing. His friends wondered how he could be so calm, but after awhile they began to sing along with him and were calmed too.

They were hailed like a triumphal procession. Nearly everyone they passed seemed to know who they were. Farmers stopped their carts and took off their hats. People working in the roadside fields halted their work to stare at the small group passing by. In every city and town of any size, crowds gathered on the streets and strained to catch a glimpse of the famous monk. At Leipzig people ran to the cart and leaned into it, trying to touch Luther. At Weimar, Justus Jonas, a good friend of Luther's, decided to join the party. At Erfurt the faculty of the university welcomed Luther as a hero at the city's gates. Town officials gave a banquet in his honor, and the Augustinians invited him and his friends to spend the night in their cloister. Many years before, Luther had lived in that same cloister as a student.

On to Eisenach, then Frankfurt, then Oppenheim. At last, on the morning of April 16, 1521, the small party neared Worms. A watchman in the cathedral tower signaled their approach with a blast of his trumpet, the city gates opened, and a crowd of people came out to meet the travelers. Inside the gates 2,000 people lined the main street, cheering Martin Luther. Many of these people did not care if there were seven sacraments or two, whether indulgences should be sold or not. What they cared about was that Luther had stood up to Rome. He was a hero to them. But Luther knew that these people were not going to decide his fate.

At four o'clock on the afternoon of April 17, 1521, the imperial herald and the imperial marshall called for Martin Luther at his room in St. John's Court and took him to the courtroom in the palace where the diet was being held. Because the streets were filled with crowds waiting to catch a glimpse of Luther, the emperor's representatives decided not to take a public route. Instead they guided Luther through secret passageways to an anteroom to wait for the time when his case would be heard. It was six o'clock, and torches had been lighted against the darkness when Luther was called to the courtroom and he and the emperor laid eyes on each other for the first time. A pile of Luther's books lay on a table at the front of the room. The secretary to the archbishop of Trier began by warning Luther not to speak unless to answer a question. Then he asked the first of the two questions that were to be put to Luther: Were these Luther's books? In a voice so soft that his listeners had to strain to hear him, Luther answered that they were.

Then came the second question: Did he defend them all, or was he ready to take them back in whole or in part?

Luther answered softly that his answer would touch God and His Word and would affect the salvation of souls, so he would like time to prepare his answer. The emperor and the diet talked it over and decided to give Luther 24 hours. Then he was led by the same secret passageways back to his quarters.

The others in the courtroom were puzzled. Many had been surprised that he had come to Worms at all and so had expected him to speak up and refuse to take back any of his teachings. He seemed so awe-struck in the courtroom that many people decided he would back down after all and that the whole problem was about to be solved.

Luther never explained why he acted so strangely at that first hearing. It is possible that he was again having doubts about the rightness of his views and actions. Even those who are close to God have times when God seems to desert them, leaving them alone and afraid. Luther's life depended on how he answered that second question, and it was no easy thing to say the words that would bring about his own death. It is also possible that he was stalling for time so as to have a wider audience. Whether or not he planned it, he did have a much larger audience the next day, for the second hearing was held before a full session of the diet, and there were so many churchmen and princes that even in the great hall of the palace it was standing room only.

Once again Luther was summoned at four o'clock, then made to wait till six. Taken before the archbishop's secretary, he heard the second question repeated. He was warned again not to make any speeches, but he cleverly got around that problem by answering that the books were not all of one sort. He then spoke for about ten minutes—in German, so perhaps he had planned this second session before a large audience after all. His writings could be divided into three groups, he said. The first were about simple faith, and even his enemies could not deny them. The second showed how the pope and his followers were destroying Germany. To deny them would be like saying, "Go ahead with your tyranny." The third attacked individuals, and maybe his language had been harsh, but he could not take them back for the same reason that he could not take back his writings against the pope. Luther ended by saying, 'If I am shown my error, I will be the first to throw my books into the fire."

The voice of John Eck strained to be heard above the loud murmurings of the crowd: Would Luther repeat what he had said in Latin? Luther did so.

His judges did not know what to do. Luther had fooled them by not giving a simple yes-or-no answer. In fact, he had challenged them to prove him wrong from the Bible. The emperor would have none of that. So he ordered the question put to Luther again and demanded a simple yes-or-no answer.

Did he or did he not take back his books? the archbishop's secretary asked.

Luther answered in Latin: "Unless I am convicted by Scripture and plain reason—I do not accept the authority of popes and councils, for they have contradicted each other—my conscience is captive to the Word of God. I cannot and I will not recant anything, for to go against conscience is neither right nor safe." Then he added in German this brief prayer: "God help me. Amen."

Immediately he was taken from the courtroom and led outside. The crowd had heard rumors that he had been arrested and put in a dungeon, so they were relieved to see him. They had heard how bravely he had spoken, and they cheered him and followed him through the streets with their arms upraised and their fingers spread in the traditional sign of victory. Luther, too, sensed victory. He doubted that a majority of the diet would vote against him. Returning to his room at St. John's Court, he told his waiting friends, "I've made it! I've made it!"

Luther was wrong. Charles V ordered the Edict of Worms, supporting the pope's ban against Luther, to be drawn up. Luther saw no reason to stay in Worms any longer. He asked the emperor if he could return to Wittenberg. Charles said he could and gave him safe conduct for 21 more days. Early the next morning Luther and his friends, led by the emperor's herald, left Worms in two carriages. Ironically they left through the town gate that was called St. Martin's.

Three days later Luther handed the emperor's herald a letter and told the man to return to Worms immediately on an urgent matter. The man did not think he should go, but Luther insisted, and the herald turned around and galloped off in the direction they had come from. Some of Luther's friends could not believe that he would send away a man who was so important to his safety, but Luther did not want to talk about it. That night, as the party was entering the woods on the outskirts of Eisenach, they were set upon by armed horsemen. Luther was pulled from the wagon and wrestled to the ground as his friends shouted and cursed the kidnappers. A horse was quickly brought around, and Luther was told to mount it. Then the horsemen and their captive disappeared into the woods.

When they were safely away and hidden by the dense

woods, the horsemen halted and dismounted. Quietly they celebrated. The kidnapping had been perfectly planned and executed. Luther, who had known about it all along, was less excited than his "kidnappers." He had been told only that his party would be ambushed and that he would be taken to a safe place. He wanted to return to Wittenberg, but he could not refuse the wishes of the man who had done so much to help him.

Fearing for Luther's safety, Frederick the Wise had told his secretary, George Spalatin, to arrange a false kidnapping. He did not want to know any details. That way he could truthfully say he knew nothing of the plot.

In the woods outside Eisenach, Luther was given a knight's clothing. Then the horsemen set off once again, taking a roundabout route so they could not be followed. At last, late in the evening, they arrived at a castle called the Wartburg, on a hill in the midst of the Thuringian Forest just south of Eisenach. It was May 4, 1521.

Sandstone monument near Altenstein, where the "attack" on Luther took place on May 4, 1521. He was taken from here to the nearby Wartburg Castle in Eisenach.

Chapter IX.
"JUNKER GEORG"

On May 6, 1521, the final draft of the edict against Luther was given to Charles V for him to sign, but he did not do so right away. Instead he said he would first get the consent of the diet. What he meant was that he would wait until he could be sure of that consent. The diet was officially over, and the members were going home. By the end of May only a minority remained, a minority who were ready to condemn Luther. The Edict of Worms was not signed and issued until May 26.

"Luther is to be regarded as a convicted heretic," the edict read in part. "When the time [21 days of safe conduct] is up, no one is to harbor him. His followers also are to be condemned. His books are to be eradicated from the memory of man." Immediately Luther's books were burned at Worms.

Luther's followers refused to accept the edict as legal, pointing out that it had been passed by a minority of the diet. Luther's enemies insisted it was legal, and the pope said it proved he was right to outlaw Luther. The pope and his advisers had not been happy that Luther's case had been heard at Worms, for the diet was not a church council. But they were willing to take any support they could get.

Meanwhile only a few people knew the whereabouts of the object of the edict, Martin Luther. All anyone else knew was that he had disappeared. The rumors flew fast and furious—he had been abducted by the pope's followers and was on his way to Rome; he had been kidnapped and murdered. Ominous rumblings came from the common people, who talked of revolution if the rumors of murder were true.

Luther did not hear much of what was going on in the outside world. He had to stay in his room at Wartburg Castle until the hair on the crown of his head grew in and his beard grew long enough to disguise his facial features. His only visitors were knights who trained him in knightly behavior, so that when he was allowed to go outside he would be able to act the way a knight should. He would be called *Junker Georg* (YOONGker GAYorg), or Knight George.

It was a painfully lonely and frightening time for him. Left alone, he realized anew the seriousness of the events in which he had become involved. Once again he wondered how he could dare to claim that he alone knew the truth. When prayer had satisfied him that he had not been wrong, he

Luther as Junker Georg. Painting by Lucas Cranach the Elder, 1522. (Kunstsammlungen zu Weimar)

worried that he had not been bold enough at Worms: he should have said more and said it more forcefully. He compared his semi-imprisonment to Christ's trials in the wilderness, and when he was allowed to write letters to a few friends, after promising not to reveal his whereabouts, he often signed them, "From the wilderness."

He found what comfort he could in work, and during the first months at the Wartburg he wrote pamphlets. He also began a new project, translating the New Testament into German. He did it without any dictionaries and finished the work in three months. If Martin Luther had done nothing else, this work alone would have assured him a place in history.

After a time Luther's beard and the hair on his head grew long enough for him to be able to go out in public. The people of the nearby town were curious to see the mysterious occupant of Wartburg Castle, but once they had seen him, their curiosity was satisfied. In his black beard and knight's clothing he looked like an ordinary knight and not very interesting. This man called *Junker Georg* went hunting in the woods, picked berries in the fields, and otherwise acted quite unmysteriously. But he did not particularly enjoy his new identity, especially the hunting part. He did not mind the idea of hunting bears and wolves and foxes for sport, but he could see no point in going after harmless creatures like rabbits. Also, even in disguise he could not move about freely. He was warned not to get friendly with or trust anyone who was not in on the plot. Though he got a lot of writing done, he was restless. "I did not want to come here," he wrote to a friend. "I wanted to be in the fray."

Back in Wittenberg quite a fray was in progress. Luther's absence did not prevent his reform movement from going ahead. Philip Melanchthon, Andreas Carlstadt, and Gabriel Zwilling, a monk of the Augustinian order, began almost immediately to make wide-reaching changes. They tried to keep Luther informed of what was happening and to seek his advice, but the medieval communication system and his being in hiding made it hard for him to know what was really going on.

He agreed to the first changes he learned about. Priests began to marry, and he thought this was right. He had written that priests should be allowed to marry, for he had

Luther's room at Wartburg Castle. The Bible containing Luther's remarks lies on the desk. On the wall are paintings of Luther's parents by Lucas Cranach the Elder and an engraving by the artist depicting Luther as Junker Joerg. The room has been preserved in its original condition.

found nothing in the Scriptures to support the traditional church teaching of priestly celibacy. When he learned that Andreas Carlstadt had married a 15-year-old girl, he was pleased. But when Carlstadt began saying that monks ought to marry too, Luther was troubled. After all, monks had made a more deliberate choice of the unmarried life than priests had. For answers he went to the Scriptures, and pretty soon he wrote a pamphlet *On Monastic Vows.* In it he stated that there was no special religious vocation, that one could serve God married as well as unmarried, leading an ordinary life as well as a monastic one. At Wittenberg monks began to leave the Augustinian order.

Carlstadt called for an end to confession, and Luther agreed that it was not necessary to confess privately to a priest in the detail commanded by the church. In a booklet titled *Concerning Confession, Whether the Pope Has Power to*

Order It, he stated his belief that too many people thought forgiveness was automatic if they confessed and that if a Christian truly repented and confessed his sins to God, he would be forgiven with or without a priest. Back in Wittenberg the common people were very much interested in this question. The matter of confession touched them closely. So did the changes in the mass that Luther's followers began to make.

Luther had written that the bread and wine at Communion should be shared with the people, just as Christ had shared these things with His disciples. In Wittenberg Luther's followers began sharing the bread and wine at Communion, saying the mass in ordinary street clothes and reciting parts of it in German.

At this point the prior of the Wittenberg cloister rebelled. Saying that he would not have the mass destroyed, he ordered that no masses at all would be celebrated in the cloister. When, on All Saints' Day, Luther's friend Justus Jonas went to the Castle Church and called all indulgences rubbish, Frederick the Wise also became angry at what he thought was too much change too fast. Everyone who clung to the old way of doing things was attacked by people like Carlstadt and Jonas. And the Augustinian monks who remained in the cloister were in fear of their lives, so bold had the students and townspeople become.

Martin Luther did not know about all this trouble. He had no idea matters had gotten so out of hand. All he knew was that he had sent several handwritten booklets to George Spalatin and that he had not seen any in published form. In mid-December 1521 he decided to make a secret trip to Wittenberg to find out why.

He arrived in Wittenberg the day after a small riot. Students and townspeople had set upon the Castle Church, taking the mass books from the altar, driving out the priests, and throwing stones at those who were praying before the statue of the Virgin Mary. Spalatin told Luther that the extreme actions of Luther's own followers had turned Frederick against the reforms. Luther was disturbed by what he found at Wittenberg and spoke out against the rioters, but Carlstadt and others told him the riots would not happen again and the situation was now in hand. He returned to the Wartburg unwillingly, knowing that while he stayed in hiding he had no control over the movement, yet if he came out of hiding he was almost sure to be arrested.

Back in Wittenberg the confusion grew more serious every day. Influenced by a group of spiritual leaders from the city of Zwickau who were against all class distinctions, all formal education, and all work except manual labor, Carlstadt began to push for even more radical reforms. He refused to be called "Doctor" anymore and went into the fields to try his hand at manual labor. On Christmas Day 1521 he said mass in a plain black robe. Although he began reading the mass in Latin, he left out all of the passages on sacrifice, and when the time came for Communion, he made a radical change. Switching from Latin to German, he offered bread and wine to all 2,000 people in the congregation, the first time the common people had ever been offered the complete Lord's Supper.

Such a radical break with tradition pleased the more adventurous in the congregation, but it frightened many others. All their lives they had been taught that the bread and wine of Communion—Christ's body and blood—were so sacred that no one but a priest could touch them. Now they were being invited to touch these sacred items, and many trembled in fright as they went up to the altar. One poor man shook so much that he dropped his piece of bread. He gazed down at what he thought was the body of Christ lying on the floor and was so ashamed that he could not bring himself to pick it up.

The smashing of idols, the beating of priests, the marrying of priests and monks and nuns, the offering of communion to everyone—all these radical changes were too much for many people. They were shaken and confused and did not know what was right and what was wrong. Frederick the Wise shared their concern. Too much was happening too fast, and he did not know who was at work in Wittenberg, God or the devil. He was also worried about the rumblings in the bordering states, where rival Saxon rulers were beginning to question Frederick's ability to control his own subjects. The bishop of Meissen asked permission to visit his domains, and Frederick reluctantly agreed, but he did not like the idea that others thought he could not keep his own house in order. When in January 1522 the Wittenberg town council passed a law calling for all remaining statues and religious images to be removed and the bread and wine to be given to all people at Communion, Frederick decided he had to take action.

On February 13 Frederick ordered that until further notice no more statues should be destroyed and no more important parts of the mass should be left out. Carlstadt should stop preaching for awhile. A period of thought and discussion was needed before any further changes were made or radical actions taken.

It was not a harsh order; it was rather a plea for reason. But the town council did not see it that way. The members saw it as a challenge to their authority, and they decided to meet that challenge. Nothing would do but to get the man back who had started it all. They wrote to Luther at the Wartburg, explaining what was happening and inviting him to return.

Luther was relieved when he got this invitation, for it gave him a clear reason to go back to Wittenberg. He was sure it was really a call from God. He wrote at once to Frederick to tell him he had decided to come out of hiding. Frederick answered with a plea to Luther to stay at the Wartburg awhile longer, warning that he could not promise to protect Luther from either the diet or the emperor; but Luther believed he had a higher protection than any the elector could offer him. He had the protection of God.

Early in March 1522 two Swiss students on their way to Wittenberg University stopped at an inn in Jena, about 60 miles east of the Wartburg, and were taken by the innkeeper into a common room occupied by a single knight. He had a bushy black beard and wore a bright red cloak and thick woolen tights. One hand held the book he was reading; the other rested on the hilt of his sword. As the students approached, he rose and, fastening his brilliant dark eyes on them searchingly for a moment, invited them to join him for a drink. They noticed with curiosity that the book he was reading was in Hebrew. The conversation soon turned to the subject that was on everyone's mind in Germany at the time—the news that Martin Luther was returning to Wittenberg. The Swiss travelers asked the knight if he knew whether Luther was in Wittenberg. "I know quite positively that he is not," the knight replied, "but he will be." The knight, of course, was Martin Luther, playing the closing scenes of his role as *Junker Georg*.

Chapter X.
THE PEASANTS' REVOLT

L uther rode hard and reached Wittenberg on March 6, 1522, just five days after he had left the Wartburg, 150 miles away. After taking over the Augustinian monastery, he told Frederick the Wise that he was back. Then he set about getting back control of the movement he had started.

He preached for eight straight days, urging moderation, patience, and consideration for others. It was wrong to force people to accept all these radical new changes, he said. The average man must be slowly and patiently educated to the new beliefs. Meanwhile, if the statues and priests' robes did not get in the way of God's truth, they should be left alone—the people still needed them.

The more radical reformers, like Andreas Carlstadt, were angered by Luther's plea for moderation. Carlstadt accused Luther of supporting the old ways and left Wittenberg to become pastor in a nearby town. The spiritual leaders from Zwickau left too, and they were as bitter against Luther as Carlstadt was. But most people were relieved to hear Luther's calm voice and reasoned arguments after months of turmoil. Before long, priests were able to go to their altars dressed in traditional robes without fear of being taunted or beaten. Mobs no longer gathered outside the churches to threaten violence against the symbols of Rome. At Communion, those who wished to take the bread and the wine did so, and those who preferred traditional Communion did not. A sense of calm settled over Wittenberg, and for the first time in months it was possible for the people to go about business as usual.

In the meantime, the news that Luther was out of hiding

spread throughout Germany and reached both Rome and Charles V. By this time Pope Leo had died, but the new pope, Adrian VI, wanted Luther punished just as much as Leo had. Charles V wanted his edict against Luther enforced; but he was busy in Spain directing a war against France. He left the matter up to the German Catholic princes. But these princes were afraid to act because Luther was so popular with the German people. There was so much unrest among the people that any action against Luther might touch off a revolution.

Of course Luther was pleased that no one tried to arrest him or punish him. But he was not pleased about the reason. The last thing he wanted was to be the cause of a revolution in Germany. In fact, his attitude toward the unrest caused some people to call him a hypocrite and a traitor.

A large group of knights used the reform cause as an excuse to wage war against the princes. Luther spoke out against the knights, even those who had been on his side at the Diet of Worms. Carlstadt began urging the peasants in his town to revolt. Frederick the Wise banished Carlstadt from Saxony, and Luther agreed it was the best thing to do. When Carlstadt heard about that, he called his former friend a papist twice over. This hurt Luther.

The social unrest continued. Monks and nuns were leaving the monasteries and convents at a high rate. In April 1523 a nun named Katherine von Bora and 11 others ran away from the Nimbschen convent in Grimma. In July 1523 two young Augustinian monks named Henry Vos and John van den Esschen left their monastery in Brussels, one of the most strongly Catholic cities in the empire. They were caught and publicly burned at the stake. The two monks were the first martyrs of the Reformation, and their deaths only caused the reform movement in Brussels to grow stronger.

All over Germany the peasants were tired of having all the religious and social and political cards stacked against them. By the early 1500s ideas of nationhood and the worth of the individual had gradually percolated down through the ranks of German society and reached the peasants, and there had been scattered revolts during the first 15 years of the century. Each time, the princes had put down the revolts quickly and with much bloodshed, and the peasants had been quiet since 1515. But the movement started by Martin Luther had gradually taken hold among them. He preached that all men were priests and that each man was responsible for his own relationship with God. The peasants decided that if this was true, they should also be treated with dignity on earth. The "ideal" social system that Charlemagne had ordered hundreds of years before just didn't work.

A new peasant revolt began in Swabia in the fall of 1524 with the publication of the *Twelve Articles of the Peasants in Swabia*. This document stated their belief in individual dignity and basic rights. The peasants were tired of paying high taxes to princes who used the money for their own power and luxury. They wanted the woods and streams to be open to everyone, not just to the princes for their own recreation. They wanted a voice in the appointment of the pastors who ministered to them. They wanted the rents on their lands reduced.

Peasants in other areas took up the cause, and the Peasants' War began. Bands of peasants began to invade the private lands, hunting in the forests and fishing in the streams. Mobs armed with pickaxes and shovels appeared before castle gates demanding fairer treatment from their landlords. When the princes refused, the mobs attacked, murdering and looting.

Luther was shocked and angered at the peasants' behavior. He understood how they felt, but he could not agree with their actions. They were threatening the basic order of society and so, in his opinion, were going against God. Luther agreed with the apostle Paul that God wanted some men to be princes and some to be peasants, so that there would be order and peace on earth. This did not mean that all princes were automatically good, but God would punish such men. If people took it on themselves to punish them, not just the rulers but the very offices of authority would be in danger. To overthrow the political and social structure would be to go against God.

Worried about the increasing strength of the peasants' revolt, Luther spoke out against the peasants. In a pamphlet called *Against the Murderous and Thieving Hordes of Peasants*, he urged the princes to put down the rebellion. It was the least reasonable writing he had yet done. He practically called for mass slaughter: "Let everyone who can, smite, slay, and stab, secretly or openly, remembering that nothing can be more poisonous, hurtful, or devilish than a rebel. It is just as when one must kill a mad dog; if you don't strike him, he will strike you, and the whole land with you."

The peasants felt betrayed. They had thought Luther was their champion. Many had even hoped he would speak to the princes on their behalf. Instead he had sided with the princes. They would never forgive him completely. Nor, for that matter, would the Catholic princes, who would always blame him for causing the revolt.

When a group of 6,000 armed peasants gathered near Frankenhausen in May 1525, the princes knew they had to act. They attacked the peasants. Over 5,000 were killed, only 600 taken prisoner. The battle at Frankenhausen signaled the end of the Peasants' War. Although there was more violence for a time, the spirit of the peasants was broken.

The war had lasted only a few months, but the destruction was unbelievable. In Thuringia 70 cloisters were demolished; in Franconia 52 cloisters and 270 castles were destroyed. The cost in human lives was much higher; about 100,000 peasants and soldiers had died. And through it all, the peasants had gained nothing. For the next three centuries they would have no say at all in the political and social life of Germany.

Martin Luther was saddened by the whole situation, but no matter how much sympathy he had for the peasants, he could not be in favor of the revolt. One reason why he had reacted so harshly to the peasants may have been that their revolt seemed to prove his enemies right. Back in the thick of his struggle with Rome they had warned: If this man is not silenced, he will soon have Germany in turmoil. Luther had always thought these attacks unfair; yet here was Germany in turmoil just as his enemies had predicted. By writing *Against the Murderous and Thieving Hordes*, he may have been trying to separate himself from the revolting peasants so he would not be blamed for their actions. He tried to soften the harshness of that pamphlet with another, published soon after, in which he urged more mercy to the peasants. But that pamphlet went practically unnoticed. What would ring in the ears of poor Germans for years to come were those words in the first pamphlet: "smite, slay, and stab." And when Luther married in June 1525, when Germany was still in complete turmoil over the Peasants' War, it seemed to many that he was dancing on the graves of the dead peasants.

Wider die Mordischen
vnd Reubischen Rotten der Bawren.

Psalm. vij.
Seyne tuck werden jñ selbs treffen/
Vñ seyn mutwill/ wirdt vber jñ außgeen.
1525.
Martinus Luther. Wittenberg.

Title page of Luther's tract against the Peasants. *Against the Robbing and Murdering Hordes of Peasants*, Wittenberg, 1525. (Lutherhalle, Wittenberg)

Chapter XI.
MARTIN
AND
KATHERINE

Luther's decision to marry was not a spur-of-the-moment idea, although he was accused of that. His marriage to Katherine von Bora came only after a great deal of thought and soul-searching about what his proper duties were to God, to Germany, and to Katherine, not to mention a bit of prodding on the part of Katherine herself.

She had been one of the 12 nuns to escape from the convent in Grimma in April 1523. While planning their escape, the nuns had contacted Luther and asked for his help. Grimma was ruled by the Saxon Duke George, who would execute anyone caught helping nuns to escape, and the nuns could find no one to help them. Luther put them in touch with a merchant who delivered barrels of herring to the convent, and one night in April the merchant left the convent with more than empty herring barrels in his covered wagon; 12 nuns were in those barrels.

Three returned to their own homes. The other nine made their way to Wittenberg, and because he had arranged for their escape, Luther felt it was up to him to get them settled and married. By November 1524 he had managed to settle six of the nuns but worried about what to do with the others. Someone suggested that he marry one himself, but he said it would be unfair to marry when he was under the emperor's ban and would quite likely be executed as a heretic. Five months later, only one nun, Katherine von Bora, remained unmarried, and Luther's good friend, George

Martin Luther, also called Luther's wedding portrait. Painting by Lucas Cranach the Elder, 1526. (Wartburg-Stiftung, Eisenach)

Katharina von Bora, Luther's wife. Painting by Lucas Cranach the Elder, 1526. (Wartburg-Stiftung, Eisenach)

Spalatin, again suggested that Luther take a wife. Once again Luther said no.

Katherine was a rather plain-looking woman with a wide, plump face and the beginnings of a double chin. Her eyes were steady and earnest and gave the impression that she saw more than she let on. Her small mouth, turned up slightly at the corners, made her look amused all the time. But she was not very happy to be 26 years old and not yet married. In those days in Germany that was almost too old for marriage. Every promising match had fallen through for one reason or another. In desperation Luther found yet another man who was willing to marry Katherine, but Katherine was not willing. Afraid that Luther would be angry and give up on her altogether, she explained that she would not take the other man, but she would take either Dr. Amsdorf of Magdeburg, who was visiting Wittenberg at the time, or Luther himself. Since both Luther, at 41, and Amsdorf were thought to be past the marrying age, she knew they would not take her suggestion seriously, but at least she had shown that she was willing to marry somebody

Luther was completely exasperated with Katherine by this time, but he laughed in spite of himself when he heard of her "proposal." On a visit to his parents in the spring of 1525 he shared the joke with them and was surprised at his father's response. Why not marry the woman? Hans Luther asked. Hans was an old man now, and since he had lost his other two sons to the plague, he worried that there was no one to carry on his name. That made Martin begin to think about the idea. Nearly all his life, it seemed, he had done battle with his father. It had been painful, because he loved his father and wanted very much to have the older man's approval. This was something he could do for his father, something that might soften the pain and hurt he had caused.

The more Luther thought about the idea, the more sensible it seemed. He did not love Katherine, but he liked her. The marriage would give Katherine status. Even if he were arrested and executed soon after, she would still have his name; and being a widow in those days was a lot better than being an old maid. It would also show that he was willing to act on his beliefs that God wanted man and woman to be together and not denied each other's company because of priestly or monastic vows.

Once Luther had made his decision, he acted on it quickly, for he knew there would be protest. He was free to marry because John von Staupitz had released him from his monastic vows seven years before, so that was not the cause of the protest. Many of his friends were not against his marrying, but they thought he could find someone better than Katherine. Others thought that Luther's marrying so soon after the slaughter of the peasants at Frankenhausen was in poor taste, but Luther would not be talked into waiting.

On June 13, 1525, Martin and Katherine were publicly engaged and the wedding was held two days later. Luther invited Dr. Amsdorf to come from Magdeburg to attend: "The rumor of my marriage is correct. I cannot deny my father the hope of [grandchildren], and I had to confirm my teaching at a time when many are so timid. I hope you will come."

Could this really be a happy marriage? Both were considered almost too old to marry. Luther was not in love with Katherine, but Katherine probably loved him or at least respected him very much; and it is just possible that she had planned to marry him all along. The marriage proved to be a solid and happy one, and Luther's wife and children would bring him great happiness and comfort over the next 20-odd years.

"There is a lot to get used to in the first year of marriage," Luther once said thoughtfully. "One wakes up in the morning and finds a pair of pigtails on the pillow which were not there before." A 41-year-old bachelor has usually become quite set in his ways, and living with a woman after all that time can take quite a bit of getting used to. In his single days Luther would leave his bed unmade and the linen unchanged for months on end; no one else would see it, and anyway, he was too busy with other things. His eating habits had been poor: he would ignore his hunger pangs if he was in the midst of some important writing, then eat too much the next day and wonder why he had digestive problems.

Katherine changed all that. He slept in a clean bed, ate regularly, wore clothes washed and patched by his new wife. He grumbled about it. Usually he called her Katie, but sometimes when he was in a grumbling mood he would change the pronunciation slightly so it came out as *Kette*, the German word for "chain." Actually he enjoyed the attention most of the time, and he came to depend on her and to respect her ideas and to worry about providing for her.

They began their marriage with no money. Katie's father did not provide a dowry, and Martin did not want to ask his father to support them. Because he was no longer a monk, he could not share in the money taken in by the Augustinian cloister; he never took any money from the sale of his books, and the small salary he got from the university was not enough to support a single person, let alone a married one. In 1526 Luther learned woodworking and installed a lathe in the cloister, hoping to be able to earn a living for himself and Katie by working as a laborer, but he never had to do that. His more well-to-do friends saw that he and his wife were provided for. Frederick the Wise gave him the whole 40-room cloister and doubled his salary. It is fitting that one of Frederick's last acts would be in support of Martin Luther, the man who had given him so much trouble but whom he had stood by to the end. Frederick died in 1525. His brother and successor, John the Steadfast, was even more generous. Others made frequent gifts of game and wine. Luther does not appear to have spent any sleepless nights worrying about money. He let Katie pay the bills that were due and figure out how to pay the next ones, and he had faith that somehow the Lord would provide, no matter how many mouths there were to feed.

Their first child, Hans, was born June 7, 1526, and was followed by Elizabeth, December 10, 1527; Magdalena, December 17, 1529; Martin, November 9, 1531; Paul, January 28, 1533; and Margaretha, December 17, 1534. In addition to all those children the Luthers took in a variety of other people over the years. What a blessing that Luther was so unconcerned about money! All the responsibility would have broken a worrying man.

Chapter XII.
REBUILDING THE CHURCH

Meanwhile a major source of the worrying Luther did do—the Edict of Worms—hung over him like a cloud. He tried to put his fate in the hands of God and not think about it too much. Although Emperor Charles V did not return to Germany for several years after the edict was issued, he did not forget about Luther, nor did the pope and the Catholic princes of Germany. Diets were held regularly without Charles—in 1522, 1523, and 1524—and at each the representatives of Charles and the pope urged the princes to act on the edict. But each time the princes could not come to an agreement. The princes who supported Luther were as strong as the Catholic princes, and the discussions always ended in a stalemate.

Some of the Catholic princes probably considered ending the whole matter by doing away with Luther themselves—and certainly the same idea occurred to those in Rome—but no one was willing to risk the political and social disorder in Germany that might result. Luther had some powerful supporters, and up until the Peasants' War he had the loyalty of a majority of the German common people.

Because of the Peasants' War no diet was held in 1525, but the Catholic princes were still active. They formed two leagues, one in the south and one in the north, to fight the spread of Lutheranism. (The terms Luther and Lutheranism were being more widely used every day, although Luther did not like it at all. Again and again he asked people to call themselves Christians instead of Lutherans. "What is Luther?" he asked. "After all, my teaching is not mine, nor have I been crucified for anyone.") The Catholic leagues told the Emperor Charles that they were prepared to act without

The elector of Saxony, John the Steadfast. Detail from a painting by an unknown artist, 16th century. In the background a representation of the battle at Frankenhausen, in which Thomas Muenzer and his followers were defeated May 15, 1525. A rainbow, a symbol of Muenzer and his followers, is shown over the battlefield. (Museum Schloss Wilhemlsburg, Schmalkalden)

the approval of any diet. Things were looking up for Charles at that time. In January 1526 he and Francis I of France signed a peace treaty that included an agreement to work together to wipe out Lutheranism and other reform movements. Charles sent word that the German princes should enforce the Edict of Worms.

But the Lutheran princes had formed their own league, the League of Torgau, and because it was every bit as strong as the two Catholic leagues, the Roman Catholic princes did not want to act unless Charles came to Germany, and this soon proved to be impossible. The peace treaty with Francis fell through, war with France was threatening again, and

Charles could not go to Germany.

All the princes attended the Diet of Speyer in the summer of 1526. Once again they talked about enforcing the Edict of Worms but could not come to an agreement. In fact, nearly every discussion ended that way—there could be no agreement on religious policies among princes who disagreed so strongly about what those policies should be. Since religious policies usually had much to do with political matters, many of those could not be decided either. The princes finally voted that until the emperor returned each German state would be free to set its own church policies. This meant that the Catholic princes could enforce Catholicism and the other princes could allow Lutheranism and other reform movements to flourish.

John the Steadfast returned to Wittenberg determined to set in order the lands he ruled. He turned immediately to Martin Luther for help, for Luther had been urging John to do something about the state of religion in Saxony since late 1525. "Everywhere the parishes are in a wretched state!" he wrote to the new elector. "No one gives, no one pays. The pennies for the souls and the sacrifices have decreased. Income has dropped or ceased altogether, so that consequently the common man respects neither the preacher nor the pastor. Unless Your Electoral Grace boldly establishes a new order and undertakes to support pastors and preachers decently, nothing will be left of the parishes, schools, or pupils. And, consequently, God's Word and the service to God will fall into ruin." So, by the time John asked him for help, Luther was ready with advice.

First a study had to be done to find out just how bad things were in the parishes and what was needed to improve matters. Then steps should be taken to make the improvements. Needed were a new organization and new institutions. The task would be difficult but exciting. Luther could hardly wait to get started on rebuilding the church the way he thought the church should be.

The electorate of John the Steadfast was divided into eight districts. With the help of his friend and fellow teacher Philip Melanchthon Luther drew up a detailed set of instructions for the men who would visit the parishes so their reports would be complete. Then he sent the visitors on their way, anxious to have their reports.

The reports were shocking. Religion everywhere seemed to be in a state of chaos. Few people really knew Luther's writings. Instead they had simply taken what they had heard, especially some of his anti-Roman ideas, and turned them into a mockery of what Luther had intended. They married without thought, did not confess their sins, drank and gambled, did not go to Communion. Many used the reform movement as an excuse to quit religion altogether. They refused to support the pastors, the monasteries and convents and schools. They did not respect their preachers—often with good reason. Many preachers knew nothing of the Scriptures or the mass; some spent their time brewing beer and showed up drunk at church.

When Luther heard how his teachings had been misunderstood and misused, he felt like giving up. But he was a fighter. He had fought the pope and the emperor, and he was not going to see his efforts wasted. If he had to do it single-handedly, he was going to see the church of his dreams become a reality in Saxony, an example to the rest of Germany and to Rome of what the church could be.

He began by saying that the schools should be separated from the churches and brought under the control of local government. His new church would not be as wealthy as the old, and it could not be expected to bear all the costs of education. The communities should support the schools. Next he turned to the problems of the pastors and preachers. They knew so little of the Bible that they could not be expected to preach worthwhile sermons. He collected his own sermons and wrote new ones and began publishing them in books for the preachers, who could use them word for word or as the basis for their own sermons.

At the same time he worked on ways to get the common people involved in religious services. One way was to make the mass meaningful to them, so he sat down and wrote out a new mass, entirely in German. It included what was good in the Catholic mass and excluded what was not true to the Scriptures. In his mass there would be a longer sermon, Communion for everyone who wanted it, and hymns to be sung not just by the pastor or choir but by the congregation as well.

Here Luther's love of music and his singing skill came into play. Since the Catholic mass did not include singing by the congregation, there were very few hymns. Luther set about writing hymns and asked his friends to do the same. Hundreds of beautiful hymns were written during the next 20 years, and some of them are still sung in Protestant churches today. Probably the most famous is "A Mighty Fortress is Our God," which has come to be called the Battle Hymn of the Reformation. If Luther had done nothing else, his hymns and his translation of the Bible into German would have caused him to be remembered.

With the help of friends he was making progress in translating the Old Testament from Hebrew into German, and it would be published in 1534. But Luther's work on the German Bible did not stop there. For the rest of his life he

A page from the *Zwickauer Gesangsbuechlein*, 1526. It shows Luther's first hymn, *"Nun freut euch lieben Christen gemein"* ("Dear Christians, let us now rejoice"). (Ratsschulbibliothek, Zwickau)

would refine it and change it. Many of the people who came to live at the cloister in Wittenberg over the years were Biblical scholars and Hebrew scholars, and it became Luther's habit to spend several hours once a week before dinner discussing with his guests the true meaning of passages that had proved difficult to translate.

While he worked tirelessly on his translation of the Old Testament, Luther realized that it would not be available to everyone for a long time and that there were many who were not educated enough to read it. So he wrote two catechisms, or explanations of the beliefs and practices he thought were basic to Christian life. Both *The Large Catechism* and *The Small Catechism* explained clearly and simply what was expected of an individual in relationship to his religion and to God. Especially *The Small Catechism* could be understood by a child and yet did not "talk down" to even the most educated adult. Both were published in 1529.

In that year the second Diet of Speyer met. Once again Emperor Charles V was not present, but he sent his brother Ferdinand to speak for him. Ferdinand was under orders to be careful at the diet, but he had his own ideas. He ordered the diet to enforce the Edict of Worms against Luther throughout Germany. The reform princes refused. By this time most of northern Germany had become Lutheran, and several states in the south, including Switzerland, had gone over to different reform movements. They were by no means united except against the Catholic states, until Ferdinand arrived in Germany. More than anything else, Ferdinand's demands united the reform princes. They voted against enforcement. Only the Catholic princes voted for it.

Ferdinand also ruled that no reform religions would be allowed in mainly Catholic states. But Catholicism could be practiced in the reform states. The Lutheran princes protested that this was not fair. If Catholic lands were to remain strictly Catholic, then Lutheran lands should be Lutheran. "We protest before God and before men that we and our people will not agree to anything in this decree that is contrary to God, to His holy Word, to our right conscience, and to the salvation of our souls," they said. From that time on, these princes were called "Protestors," or "Protestants," and the term Protestant was used to describe any Christian church that did not agree with the Roman Catholic Church.

107

Chapter XIII.
THE AUGSBURG CONFESSION

Many of the reform princes were angry and frustrated after the Second Diet of Speyer. Philip of Hesse, for one, decided that if the reform princes were to have any power they would have to present a solid front. Even before the diet, he had started talking with reformers in France and Bohemia, long-time enemies of the Saxon princes. The Saxons had been horrified at this and were worried that Germany would be even more divided than it already was. But after the second Diet of Speyer they agreed that something had to be done.

A number of questions of faith separated the Lutherans and the Swiss reformers, who were led by Ulrich Zwingli. Martin Luther did not like the idea of even talking about a political alliance based on religious matters, but he reluctantly agreed to meet with a group of German and Swiss religious experts at Philip's castle in October 1529. Philip hoped that a concordance, or agreement, on religious matters could be reached there, but no such agreement came about. Luther would not compromise; the truth was the truth, and no one could change it. Philip pleaded that at least they could unite to defend the right of each to his own beliefs even if those beliefs were not the same. Luther was able to agree to that, but that small agreement was not enough for the kind of alliance Philip of Hesse was after. The Lutherans and the Swiss reformers went their separate ways. Two years later Zwingli was killed in a battle. One year later Martin Luther was forced to go into hiding again.

The reason was the return of Charles V after a nine-year absence. After defeating Francis I of France, he was at last free to give his full attention to troublesome Germany and its religious problems. He arrived in Germany in 1530 and announced to the Diet of Augsburg that he was going to settle the question of religion once and for all.

Luther wanted to go to Augsburg and appear before the emperor. In fact, he set out for Augsburg in early April with a party that included Elector John the Steadfast, Philip Melanchthon, and George Spalatin. But on their arrival at Coburg Castle on April 15, the elector told Luther he could not go any farther. He was still under imperial ban, and to go to Augsburg or anywhere outside Saxony would be like committing suicide. So Luther went into hiding once again, this time for six months, frustrated at the idea that others were fighting his battle for him. During this time his father died, and he was saddened that he could not have been with the older man before his death. But he was pleased by other reports. In his absence the practice of religion in Saxony went on as if he had been right there in Wittenberg. He had laid a

Philip of Hesse. A painting attributed to Hans Krell, 1525-30. (Wartburg-Stiftung, Eisenach)

solid foundation for the reformed church, and it did not fall apart without him. He only hoped that Melanchthon and the others at Augsburg would uphold the faith as well.

At Augsburg each religious group was called on to write a statement of its basic beliefs. It was hoped that perhaps these beliefs, when set down on paper, would not prove to be too much different from the doctrines of Rome. John the Steadfast wanted a statement to come from Saxony alone, and he asked Philip Melanchthon to write it. Melanchthon took a long time to do so. Some people thought him timid and cowardly because he seemed to delay in writing the statement. But Melanchthon just wanted to do the right thing. He did not want to be responsible for bringing about a definite break in the church. He still hoped some way could be found to reform the Catholic Church from within. He wrote to Luther for advice several times, and Luther's answers were helpful and not critical.

Ulrich Zwingli. Engraving by Rene Boyvin after a painting by Hans Asper, 1531. (Kunstsammlungen zu Wiemar)

City of Augsburg. The imperial diet of 1530 took place in this building. The festivities were held on the first floor at the right.

The first drafts of Melanchthon's statement talked mainly about the abuses in the church and the right of the princes of Saxony to correct those abuses in their own areas. But when other reformist statements were published, and they all stressed differences in basic beliefs, Melanchthon felt he had to include arguments about Lutheran faith and doctrine. His final draft was such a clear and forthright statement that many other princes and representatives asked if they could add their signatures to it. John the Steadfast reluctantly agreed. He also agreed to join the other princes in demanding that the statement be given a public reading. On June 25, 1530, the document that came to be known as the Augsburg Confession was read in public.

During all his labors Philip Melanchthon had never dreamed that he would write the first public statement of the Lutheran and therefore of the Protestant faith. Luther was

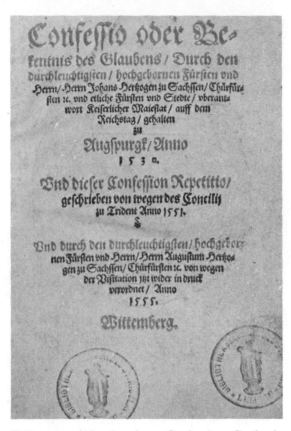

Title page of the Augsburg Confession, *Confessio Augustana invariata*, 1530. Wittenberg, 1555. (Universitaetsbibliothek, Karl-Marx-Universitaet, Leipzig)

less surprised than his friend. He was almost certain that there was no hope for unity with the Roman Catholics. If war resulted, as Melanchthon feared, so be it. Whatever happened would be God's will, and God would protect the true believers.

Charles V didn't want to let the Augsburg Confession go unanswered, so he ordered John Eck (who had debated Luther on behalf of the Catholic Church back in Leipzig) and other Catholic priests and professors to prepare a statement that would expose all errors in the Confession. A statement that Charles could accept was not ready until August 3. It did not prove the Lutherans wrong in the way they understood the Scriptures; all it did was prove that their doctrines disagreed with those of the established church and repeat that if they did not give up most of their beliefs and return to the church, the emperor would act.

The Lutherans refused to accept the statement and drafted a defense of their Confession. Charles did not know what to do. The Turks were threatening the empire, and the last thing he wanted was a divided Germany. He desperately wanted to get the two factions back together. At the same time he did not want to appear weak. So once again he delayed. Finally, in mid-September, he issued an ultimatum: the Lutherans and other reformers were to return to the Roman Catholic Church no later than April 15, 1531. Meanwhile they were not to print or sell any more books about their beliefs or try to win any more converts or prevent any Catholics from practicing their beliefs.

Although the Diet of Augsburg did not end until November, the reformers left right after Charles issued his ultimatum. John the Steadfast and his party left Augsburg on September 23 and went to Coburg, where they picked up Luther. Then they all went on to Wittenberg. On the way back, and for days after their return, Luther questioned those who had been at Augsburg about what had happened there. It had been very difficult for him to stay at Coburg while such important business was going on. He wasn't surprised that the conflict between the Roman Church and the reform movement had not been cleared up, but he was frustrated. As long as the conflict hung in the air, so did his own position. But he was beginning to realize that uncertainty about his safety was a cross he would always have to bear. He spent the rest of his life under the ban of both Rome and the emperor.

Luther was not the only one who was frustrated. The Lutherans and other reformers were frustrated too—about Luther. Since they were not going to return to the Roman Catholic Church on April 5, 1531, they knew they had better try to reach some agreement among themselves so they could present a united front if a showdown came. But every time they tried, Luther would refuse to compromise. He knew what was at stake, but he stuck to the belief for which he had gone through so much pain and suffering: the Gospel was something that could not be changed because of circumstances. He had seen the Roman Church, the princes, and the peasants use it for their own ends. He did not want it exploited by his own people.

There were some very real disagreements among the

reformers. One of the most serious concerned the Lord's Supper. The non-Lutherans in southern Germany and Switzerland did not believe that Christ's body and blood are really present in the sacrament and eaten and drunk by the communicants; the bread and wine could not possibly be the body and blood of Christ up in heaven. Bread and wine, they said, could only symbolize, or represent, Christ's body and blood. Luther insisted that Jesus had said, "This *is* My body; this *is* My blood," and so it must be true even if we cannot see how. As long as such disagreement remained, Luther could not imagine any joining with the other reform movements.

Luther's own supporters thought him stubborn and shortsighted. How could he be so stubborn when the future of the reform movement was at stake? Melanchthon and the others continued their talks with the non-Lutherans in spite of him. The result was the formation of the League of Schmalkald in February 1531. It did not represent an agreement on matters of faith, but it did produce a mutual promise among most of the evangelical states and cities to come to one another's defense in the event of an attack. The league was strong enough to cause Charles V to think twice about moving against the reformers. April 15 came and went, and no one acted. The reformers ignored the deadline, and Charles made no move to enforce his ultimatum of the previous September.

The Reformation was beyond the control of Martin Luther, and he did not like this at all. It was not a matter of ego; he did not claim to have started the movement, and he urged his followers not to call themselves Lutherans. But he believed that because of his years of Bible study and soul-searching he knew what God wanted and what He did not want, and he believed it was his duty to remain true to God, no matter what the consequences.

He continued to study and write, but his writings were no longer as popular as they had once been. The man who had almost single-handedly taken on the Roman Catholic pope was now scorned as "the pope of Wittenberg." In response, he became even more bad-tempered. He wrote savage attacks against those who would compromise the truth for any reason at all. The language of some of these writings is almost embarrassing to those who would speak of God and religion only in high-toned terms. Luther saw no reason not to get down to the nitty-gritty, and he enjoyed shocking those with delicate sensibilities.

One of his favorite stories was about the time St. Augustine was asked where God was before heaven was created. Augustine had answered that God was in Himself. Luther said that when the same question was put to him, he replied, "God was creating hell for idle, presumptuous fools such as you!"

In Luther's opinion, talking about God in pretty language was to deny God's presence on earth and His power to affect the affairs of men. He could and did speak of God in

Luther House in Schmalkalden. Luther was ill when the Protestant princes came to Schmalkalden for a meeting of the league in 1537. Therefore Luther received his guests on the third floor of this building dating back to the beginning of the 16th century. Among the guests were Ulrich, duke of Wuerttemberg; Philip of Hesse; Melanchthon; Spalatin; Bugenhagen; and Justus Jonas.

"barroom" language when he was addressing people he thought were hypocrites. In doing so he was probably ahead of his time. He certainly did not know a great deal about psychology as we know it. He did not use psychological terms, like "denial," that we do today; but he understood how people's minds work. Nowadays we learn that by talking of death as "passing away" we are refusing to deal with death, to face the fact of death. If we really faced it, we would say, "He is dead," not "He passed away." So also with other subjects we are not comfortable with: the more uncomfortable we are with a subject, the more politely we talk about it. Back in the 1530s and 1540s Martin Luther was saying the same thing: If you are really in touch with God, you do not need to be polite. Nowadays that "crotchety old man" would probably have been much more respected than he was then.

When Luther faced God alone, in private, he wrote poetry. He was still writing hymns. He was still working on his translation of the Bible, which was a sort of poetry in itself. Although he had completed and published one translation, he would continue to refine and perfect it until his death. When he was with his family and friends he gave some of the most inspiring lectures ever recorded in the history of Christianity. Down-to-earth though they were, there was a great beauty in their simplicity, like the proverbs of common people the world over.

He gave many of these lectures not in classrooms but in his own dining room. There was lots of space in the 40-room cloister, and one of the ways Luther and Katie made ends meet was to take in student boarders. They ate with the family at dinnertime, and since Luther enjoyed holding forth at the dinner table, they began to see the dinner hour as extra class time and brought notebooks. Katie grumbled that they should pay for this extra teaching, and Luther himself did not like the idea of having to be the wise professor at a time when he should be relaxing and enjoying the company of family and friends, but he never put a stop to it.

Later generations have been grateful to those students with their thirst for knowledge and their habit of taking notes. After Luther's death these students organized the 6,000-plus entries in their notebooks, and Luther's *Table Talk* is one of the most complete collections of the thoughts and opinions of a famous man.

Chapter XIV.
THE LAST YEARS

Luther did not lose his popularity completely after 1530. He was still respected. The Lutherans may have thought him stubborn and ill-tempered, but they still went to him for help when they needed a written statement of the reform movement's beliefs. And so, in December 1536, it was Luther whom Elector John Frederick the Magnanimous, ruler of Saxony after his father John the Steadfast died in 1532, asked to draw up a statement for the reformers to present to a general church council. Back in 1533 the new pope, Paul III, had decided on such a meeting. After much delay, it seemed toward the end of 1536 that a council might be held in the Italian city of Mantua in May 1537. The League of Schmalkald wanted to be ready.

Luther went right to work. The elector, perhaps thinking of Luther's habit of using coarse language, asked that Luther set down in *godly* writing the beliefs and thoughts he would be prepared to stand on at his death, and this is what Luther did. Barely two weeks and eighteen pages later, Luther became too ill to write, but he continued to dictate his articles, and they were ready in rough form to be discussed during the Christmas holidays by Melanchthon, Spalatin, and others. They were submitted in final form to John Frederick on January 3, 1537. "These are the articles on which I must stand," said Luther, "and, God willing, shall stand even to my death. I do not know how to change or surrender anything in them." At that time Luther believed he was near death, so these were not idle words.

By February, he was feeling better and went with John Frederick and others to the Diet of Schmalkald, where the articles were to be discussed. But at Schmalkald he became ill again and so could not defend his articles, which came right out and said that a split had taken place in the church, one that might never be mended. At the discussions Philip Melanchthon pleaded for the delegates to rest their case on the Augsburg Confession, which did not actually discuss a break with Rome. The delegates took Melanchthon's advice, and Luther's Schmalkald Articles were never actually discussed as policy but merely signed by those present. But they were soon known throughout Germany anyway and were to be very important in the later unification of the reform churches.

Luther seemed to be near death in early 1537, but he miraculously began to recover, and throughout Germany people cried, "Luther lives!" For all his crotchetiness and stubbornness Luther was still the man who had stood up to the pope and the emperor. He was a symbol of the Reformation.

Some of his enemies thought he was really dead and that his followers were saying he was alive because they knew how powerful a symbol he was. Luther took great glee in writing a pamphlet proving he was alive. "I assure you that I am living," he wrote. "To the great disgust of the devil, the pope, my enemies, and myself." He was tired of living, for he suffered from a variety of ailments and was continually plagued by sickness. He did not like the way the Reformation was going, and since he could not control it, at times he preferred to be out of it altogether. His greatest joy in his last years was not in religious matters or reforming the world but in his family and home life.

In spite of his constant complaints, he was a loving father and husband. He loved and respected his wife, Katie, who held her own with him and never let him lord it over her. At one point, for example, Luther began to lecture on his struggles with the devil. He went on about them so much that his listeners started to feel guilty because they had never had such struggles. One night Katie got up from the dinner table without a word, went to her room, and fainted. Afterward she announced in Latin that she too had been visited by the devil but had managed to overcome him. From then on her husband did not speak in superior tones about his struggles with the devil, at least not to her.

He also loved his children, especially his second daughter, Magdalena, born in 1529. He was keenly interested in all his children's thoughts and opinions and tried hard to respect them, hoping in that way to protect them from the unhappiness of his own childhood. If his various ailments caused him to be grouchy at times, he made a point of giving his children special attention at other times, to make up for it. As his family grew and developed, he probably decided he had done a much better job of it than he had in reforming the Roman Church.

In 1539 Luther himself added to the troubles of the reform movement. Landgrave Philip of Hesse, the man who had worked so hard to bring about unity among the various reform churches, had at age 19 married Christina, daughter of Duke George of Saxony, in a politically arranged match. He did not love his wife and looked for love outside marriage for awhile, but after his conversion to the reform movement he had started to feel guilty. If he had still been a Catholic, he might have gotten the pope to annul, or erase, his marriage, but as a Lutheran he could not go to the pope. He had fallen in love with 17-year-old Margaret of Saale, but what was he to do? His advisers suggested that he take a second wife. After all, Abraham and other Old Testament figures had more than one wife. Christina and Margaret agreed to the idea. So did Margaret's mother, so long as Philip could get statements from some learned men that having two wives was not against God's will. So Philip sent a representative to Wittenberg to talk with Luther and Melanchthon.

This was not the first time Philip had confessed his problem to Luther. He had been wrestling with his conscience for years. But now that he had fallen in love with Margaret, he was desperate. Luther knew very well that God never meant a man to have more than one wife. People like Abraham and Jacob had more than one wife; and others took in the widows of dead relatives and friends. But the Scriptures said very clearly, "The twain [two] shall be one flesh." Yet Philip insisted that the whole situation was making him ill, and finally Luther and Melanchthon agreed that if he absolutely had to, he should marry Margaret. But they warned him to keep the whole matter secret. If it ever became public, people would know that Philip thought he did not have to obey the same laws they did. Luther and Melanchthon were not proud of giving Philip their permission, but it seemed the only thing to do under the circumstances.

But Margaret's mother would not go along wth a secret marriage. The ceremony was performed in public and caused a scandal. Philip had broken the law, and people like Luther and Melanchthon had agreed to it. Philip was forced to beg Emperor Charles for mercy, and this weakened the Protestant alliance. Melanchthon and Luther were quite embarrassed. Melanchthon became physically ill over the whole thing. Luther did not become any more ill than he was already, but he was very angry with Philip. He never would have agreed to a public ceremony. He could not explain why he had agreed to the second marriage because the things Philip had said and written to him were said to him as a confessor, and he was bound to keep silent about them.

From then on, Luther did not have much sympathy for men with marriage problems. For that matter, he wasn't very sympathetic to anyone except his family and friends. Plagued by illness, he became more and more sour and unwilling to bear the burdens he felt God had placed on him. The death of his favorite daughter, 13-year-old Magdalena, in 1542 was a severe blow he never fully recovered from. Yet when he was called on for help, he managed to rise to the occasion.

In spite of his reputation for being ill-tempered, Luther was known as an excellent problem-solver, and when a dispute arose between the counts of Mansfeld, Luther was asked to help settle the problem. The message came in January 1546. Katie was against her husband's making the hard journey to Eisleben in the dead of winter. She wanted him to wait until spring, but he insisted he was well enough to go then.

On January 23, 1546, Luther, his sons Martin and Paul, and several friends set out for Eisleben. They were slowed by the cold winds and deep snow, and when they reached Halle, they found the Saale River too full of ice to cross. While waiting for the ice to break up, Luther wrote to his wife: "Dear Katie, don't worry about me. Read your Bible and remember that God is almighty. He could create ten Dr. Martins if the old one were drowned in the Saale. Dismiss your cares, for I have One who cares for me better than you and all the angels can."

Within a few days the ice on the river had broken up enough for a boat to cross. The party made the crossing safely, but before they reached Eisleben, Luther fell ill, and so the first meetings to solve the problems between the counts were held without him. He soon felt better and was able to attend the meetings and to preach four times at Eisleben. Within three weeks he had helped the counts reach a legal and honorable settlement, and on February 17 he and they signed an accord, sealing the agreement.

That evening after dinner, Luther complained of pains in his chest and went to bed early. Worried, his sons and friends stayed up, looking in on him now and then, comforting him when he spoke to them but remaining silent otherwise, for they saw that he was praying. At about 2 a.m. he had a second attack, but he continued to pray. After the third attack Luther's friend Justus Jonas sensed that the end was near. "Reverend father," he asked, "are you willing to die in the name of the Christ and the doctrine which you have preached?" "Yes!" said Luther in a strong voice. Then he fell asleep for the last time, in the town where he had been born and baptized. He was 62 years old.

A funeral service was held the next day in St. Andrew's Church in Eisleben. Then Luther's tin coffin was placed on a

Luther in death. Drawing by Lucas Furtenagel, 1546. (Lutherhalle, Wittenberg)

horse-drawn wagon for the journey back to Wittenberg. The procession, which included a large escort of princes and soldiers and friends, had to make its way slowly along the rough roads, for the news of Luther's death had traveled quickly, and hundreds of people came to pay their last respects. At times the procession had trouble moving at all, so thick were the crowds. Four days later the cortege arrived in Wittenberg. Luther's coffin was carried into the Castle Church through the very door on which he had nailed his *95. Theses* 30 years earlier. After a funeral ceremony his body was lowered into a crypt in the floor in front of the pulpit. Martin Luther, the man, was no more, but his memory would live on and on.

The house in which Luther died in Eisleben, the city of his birth. View from the courtyard. It is located adjacent to St. Andrew's Church and dates back to the beginning of the 16th century.

Chapter XV.
THE LEGACY OF
MARTIN LUTHER

Luther's death did not make much difference to the Protestant Reformation. The movement had long ago stopped depending on a single man, and it was spreading quickly. Religious reform was an idea whose time had come in Europe in the 16th century. Even the Catholics realized this, or at least most of them did, including the new pope. The Council of Trent would order several changes in church practice. But by the time the general church council met in Trent, Italy, in 1545, the Protestants were no longer involved in questions of Catholic Church reform. The split with the Catholic Church had become final by then.

The Council of Trent did not end until 1563, nearly 20 years after it started, so it did not decide any of the major issues that divided Germany and much of the rest of Europe. The major decisions came at other meetings. In 1555, at another Diet of Augsburg, the Edict of Worms was repealed. So the ban against Martin Luther was lifted at last, nine years after his death. At this same meeting the princes agreed to continue allowing reform states to practice reform religions and Catholic states to practice Catholicism. Germany was officially divided on religion, but by this time the reform movement had gone far beyond Germany, into Sweden, Denmark, Norway, Iceland, and Poland, not to mention such areas as Belgium and Switzerland, where it had started much earlier.

There were threats of war. In 1538 the Catholic League of Nuernberg had made such a threat, but a truce was worked out at Frankfurt the following year. In 1540 and 1541 there were further talks, but a final peace seemed impossible. War between the Catholic League of Nuernberg and the Protestant League of Schmalkald finally did break out, and the League of Schmalkald lost. But the reformers gained new strength after the powerful Catholic prince, Maurice of Saxony, went over to the Protestant cause.

In the Treaty of Passau in 1552 the Catholic states agreed not to attack the Protestant states anymore, and the Religious Peace of Augsburg of 1555 officially recognized the reform churches. But several parts of that were not clear, and it was not until 1648, over a century after Luther's death, that the Peace of Westphalia recognized the existence of the Protestant churches, and the threat of war ended at last.

At an earlier time in history, large-scale war might have broken out over this split in the church. But in the 16th century there were so many other wars going on, so many explorations into the New World, so much interest in trade with the East and worry over attempts by the Ottoman Turks to stop that trade that the Catholic princes of Europe, not to mention Rome itself, did not have either the time or the desire to concentrate on stamping out the Reformation. Then too, ideas of nationhood were emerging in Europe, and though Rome might have wished to wipe out the Protestants and end the split in the church, it no longer had the power to do so. In spite of years of hostility, the reform movement flourished after Luther's death.

The part of the reform movement that had come to be called Lutheranism continued to be plagued by infighting for another 30 years after Luther died. There were two major factions, the Philippists, named after Philip Melanchthon and centered in Wittenberg, and the "Genuine Lutherans," based in Jena. Over the years representatives of the two factions met many times to try to work out their disagreements and unite. At last, in 1577, a settlement was made that pleased the majority of churches in both factions. The Formula of Concord (Agreement) was published in the Book of Concord in 1580, the 50th anniversary of the Augsburg Confession, and 400 years ago this year, 1980. Although not all Lutheran churches accepted the Formula of Concord, that agreement is considered the beginning of unified Lutheranism.

The Book of Concord contains the official teaching of the Lutheran Churches, including the Augsburg Confession,

Title page of the *Book of Concord*, Dresden, 1580. (Evangelisches Pfarramt St. Andreas-Nicolai, Eisleben)

Luther's Schmalkald Articles, and his Small and Large Catechisms. It sets forth the major beliefs and doctrines of Lutheranism, and these remain largely unchanged today:

People are born selfish beings who neither love nor fear God. Since God knows this, He sent His own Son to be a man on earth. People can understand Christ, because He lived as a man. All God asks is that people believe in the Gospel, that Christ was sent to die for man's sins, and put their faith in Christ. The Scriptures are the Word of God and the "sole rule of faith and practice."

The churches we see are human institutions, and so they can be weak and sinful. But God works in them through His Word and the sacraments.

Two sacraments are recognized as ordained by God: Baptism and the Lord's Supper. Formal private confession is not necessary in the Lutheran Church. As to the Lord's Supper, Luther's view that Christ's body and blood are really present in the bread and wine won out over the idea that the bread and wine are just symbols.

The Lutheran churches see church and state as separate (so Lutherans understood the separation of church and state in the U.S. Constitution when it was drafted), but they do not see the state as completely separate from God. Through the state God rules man's outward actions; through the church He rules man's heart. Ideally, church and state should exist side by side and help each other, but neither should be under the control of the other.

Saved by faith in Christ, believers live to His glory by doing their best in their everyday jobs—at home, in school, at work.

Although every baptized Christian is a priest because he belongs to the universal priesthood of believers, public preaching and the administration of sacraments are done by ministers who have been "called" to special duty by God and their congregation.

Worship services are called "services" everywhere except in Sweden, where they are called "masses." Services are conducted in the language of the people. Sermons about the Biblical way of salvation are very important, and so are hymns, sung by the entire congregation. Communion, or the Lord's Supper, is celebrated at least once a month in many churches.

Four rites are recognized by the Lutheran Church: confirmation, ordination, marriage, and burial. Children are usually confirmed between the ages of ten and fifteen; at that time they make a public statement of the faith they received when they were baptized. Marriage may either replace a civil ceremony or bless a civil ceremony. Ordination does not give a minister special status (he may marry and he may be removed from office); but it does entitle him to his parishioners' respect because of the office. There is no sacrament of extreme unction, but there is a burial service for the dead.

To sum up, the Book of Concord and the practices of the Lutheran Church agree in all important ways with the teachings and ideas of Martin Luther. He never gave up his hope that a break with the Catholic Church might be avoided and that the reform movement would do just as its name suggests—reform the Catholic Church. In fact, he did help to bring about reforms in that church, but they came too late and did not go far enough. The Council of Trent, which began in 1545 and ended in 1563, agreed to a general clean-up of abuses, such as the sale of indulgences, and to the establishment of seminaries so that priests would be better educated. These were some of the reforms that Luther had talked about, but by the time these policies were formally agreed on, he had been dead 17 years.

Even though he did not want people to call themselves Lutherans, Luther would probably have been pleased with the development of the church that bears his name, and he would have been absolutely amazed at the size of that church today. With more than 75 million members, it is the largest of the Protestant churches and can be found throughout the world, on all the continents and on the islands of the seven seas.

Martin Luther would probably also have been pleased about a recent development in the United States. Since 1965 representatives of the Lutheran Church and the Roman Catholic Church have met several times. They have talked about each other's beliefs and teachings to see on what points they can agree and on what points they still differ. The hope is, of course, that the major differences between the two churches might someday be resolved.

Luther believed, and Lutherans believe, that God in His Word is the final authority and that any man, no matter how close to God, even if he is the pope, can be wrong. Catholics believe that when the pope is speaking as the official representative of the church in matters of faith and doctrine he cannot make mistakes. Luther believed, and Lutherans believe, that people need only have faith in Christ to be saved. Catholics do not believe that mere faith in Christ is enough for salvation, but a person must also perform deeds of love to make himself acceptable to God.

These are serious differences, and the two churches may never be able to erase them. If Luther were alive today, he would be excited about the possibility that they could be erased (he never wanted to cause a complete break with the Catholic Church). But he would probably be just as stubborn about not compromising as he was when the reform churches tried to unite, and when his refusal to go along with the Catholic Church teachings of his day put his life in danger. He didn't go through all that pain and trouble to have the results of his efforts wiped out 400 years later.

But history has a way of passing by even those who help to make it. Christopher Columbus, once he had discovered the New World, wanted to govern it, or at least the rich lands we now call Latin America. He turned out to be a very poor governor, and the king and queen of Spain had to remove him. In his last year he suffered from ill health (arthritis) and frustration just as Martin Luther did. But Luther no doubt died happier than Columbus, because the discovery Luther made could never be taken away from him. Martin Luther will always have his gracious God. Even in his grouchiest moments he never lost sight of his belief that God is the final authority, and so he would not insist on approving any plans for Lutherans and Catholics to talk about their differences and maybe someday reunite. If it were possible to ask him, he would probably say, "It is not my approval that you need, but God's in His Word."